Haunted

A GUIDE TO
PARANORMAL
IRELAND

PAUL FENNELL

POOLBEG

Published 2006
by Poolbeg Press Ltd
123 Grange Hill, Baldoyle
Dublin 13, Ireland
E-mail: poolbeg@poolbeg.com
www.poolbeg.com

© Paul Fennell 2006

Copyright for typesetting, layout, design
© Poolbeg Press Ltd

The moral right of the author has been asserted.

1 3 5 7 9 10 8 6 4 2

A catalogue record for this book is available from the British Library.

ISBN 1-84223-286-X
ISBN 978-1-84223-286-6

Typeset by Patricia Hope in Sabon 11/15
Printed by Litografia Rosés, S.A, Barcelona, Spain

Haunted

Contents

Introduction

Do you believe in ghosts? What if you are in a house and you hear footsteps in the room above you . . . and you are alone? What if you sense the presence of another person in the room with you? Do you tell yourself it is a figment of your imagination or something real? By "ghost" we usually mean the spirit of a dead person that can still be heard or seen on earth. So, ghost is in fact the wrong word to use; until you know exactly what is haunting you.

A "ghost" is in fact simply residual energy or the playback of some event in the past.

A "spirit" is the soul of the person that has chosen to remain behind or comes back to visit. To dismiss ghosts, spirits and the paranormal as figments of your imagination, when haunting and sightings are so common that thousands of people have stories to tell, is surely sweeping your own beliefs under the rug.

My name is Paul Fennell and I am a paranormal researcher and investigator.

My first introduction to the paranormal occurred when I was just a few months old. I was born in 1964 in a corporation house on the outskirts of Dublin in Crumlin, the youngest of a family of five brothers and two sisters. Shortly after I was born my mother was told that I had pneumonia and to enjoy the short time she would have with me. I had only a few weeks to live. I was just three months old and lay in my cot in the front room of my family home. Around it stood my older brothers and sisters. My mother was in the kitchen preparing the evening meal for my father when he returned from work.

My family's account of what happened next is as follows. There was a knock on the door. One of my brothers answered the door to a monk dressed in brown and cream clothing with a thick rope tied around his waist. He brushed my brother aside, walked into the house and straight over to my cot. Standing over me he blessed me and touched my forehead with his hand. My brothers' and sisters' screams alerted my mother to the stranger who had just walked into our house and was now at my cot.

She ran from the kitchen just as he left through the front door. She followed him demanding to know who he was and what he was doing in our house, but he had vanished. She searched down the side of the house and up and down the street but he was gone. Who this monk was or where he came from no-one knows. One thing is certain I survived the bout of pneumonia and I am now married with a beautiful wife and two beautiful daughters. I am about to celebrate my 42nd birthday and I am always grateful to this monk and though I have long searched for an answer to this question, I have not found it . . . yet.

My paranormal happenings resumed when I was in my early teens. Lying asleep one night, in the same bedroom in which I was born, I was woken by the sensation of someone sitting on the end of my bed. My bedroom was always illuminated by a street lamp just outside the house. Looking at the end of my bed I expected to see my mother or one of my brothers (with whom I shared a room) but nobody was there. I did, however, see the black cloud-like figure of a person. I could not make out if it was male or female, I just knew it was there and facing me. My knees shot up into my chest and as I pulled them in harder I could hear and feel my heart pounding in my chest. I tried to let out a scream but could only make the sound in my mind. I stayed like this for about 10 minutes until I started to realise that if it wanted to hurt me it would have done so by now. I began to relax a little but kept a steady stare on the figure sitting on my bed. After what seemed like an eternity the figure raised itself from my bed. I could feel the end of the bed lift as it moved up into a standing position. It continued to look at me for a few more seconds until it turned and just dissipated into nothing. I did not sleep a wink all night wondering if it would return, neither did I tell any of my family just in case they thought I had flipped.

This incident in my childhood left such a mental scar that the hairs still rise on the back of my neck, even today as I write this. From that day on the happenings in my mother's house became more frequent. These would include the temperature dropping in a room in the middle of a hot

PAUL FENNELL

summer's day or a dark shadow passing by the opened door of my bedroom. Often, I would come down the stairs to hear a female voice call out my name in a whisper "Paul" knowing at the time I was alone in the house. The first time I heard this I took nearly the full flight of stairs in one step. Another strange occurrence happened one night while all the family were watching television. My brother was drinking a cup of tea. Too lazy to bring the cup back into the kitchen he put it on the mantlepiece just over the fireplace. All seemed fine until the cup suddenly flew off the mantlepiece and onto the floor. We looked at one another. Nothing was said but we knew by looking at each other's faces that this was not the first time that any of us had encountered strange happenings. Later that night I plucked up the courage to tell my brothers about my strange experiences and to my relief their experiences were nearly identical to mine.

As I entered my late teens like most lads I took up sport. My chosen sport was martial arts. I also bought a set of weights to do some weight training in my bedroom. I used to keep my weights neatly piled up against the wall of my bedroom just in case my mother tripped over them. On this particular day I was taking a shower on the ground floor. The only other people in the house were my mother and one of my brothers. They heard and could feel the ceiling above banging and heaving from my weight lifting. I could also hear the noise but thought it was my brother playing around with the weights. It was not until I walked out of the shower that my mother and brother shot me a look. I knew immediately what they were thinking. If Paul was in the shower then who was using the weights upstairs? My

4

brother and I sprinted up the stairs into my room only to see my weights scattered around the floor. I knew this was not possible, as I had just tidied them up before having my shower.

It was not only my family who experienced these strange events but also my wife who was then my girlfriend. Deciding to stay overnight I fixed a bed for her on the settee. I kissed her goodnight and went to bed. In the morning she asked me what I wanted her for after I went to bed. I looked puzzled at her. 'What do you mean,' I asked? 'Shortly after you went to bed you called me. I heard it clearly, you called my name.' I had not but in the back of my head I knew what was happening. Whatever was in my house had made itself known to Angie by calling her name. It was letting her know that it was in the house. The spirit presence in my mother's house continued to make itself known even after I eventually got married and moved out. It still continues to make itself known to this day.

These incidents left me with a great interest in and respect for the paranormal, as did the presence of the monk, throughout my life. I truly believe in its presence, as a couple of times during my life I have been in danger and something has intervened to keep me safe.

Some years later I was sitting at my computer when I felt compelled to type in the words, Paranormal Ireland. Several sites appeared but one in particular stood out: Paranormal Research Association of Ireland. I made contact, joined and was invited to an open investigation at Charleville Castle, Tullamore, Co. Offaly. A few days later after a two hour drive we arrived at the long winding driveway to the

Castle. I was in awe of its splendour and couldn't wait for nightfall. I was introduced to the owners, Dudley and Bonnie. They made me feel at home and we headed to the kitchen for a cup of tea and a chat around a huge open fire. Dudley explained that he did not charge the group for investigations and that we helped him work on the castle in return for the night's stay and investigation. I have never been afraid of manual labour and looked forward to the work as a bonus on top of the investigation. We set up our equipment in the octagonal room of the castle, a room that was to become our base room on many visits. At about 5:30pm we headed down to the village to get provisions for the night ahead. By 7pm that evening I was sitting down to a meal at the main banquet table of the castle feeling like the lord of the manor. By the time the meal was over it was dark, perfect ghost hunting conditions. We had a pre-investigation meeting where the rules of investigating a location were explained to me. I also learned how to use paranormal investigation equipment. I felt somewhat unprepared as everyone else in the group had an array of technical equipment and all that I was armed with was a 35mm camera. I was handed a two-way radio just in case I got separated from the group or needed to report an incident. With excitement running through my body we headed off into the darkness of the castle corridors. It was not long before things became interesting. Members of the group began to capture suspected orbs on their digital cameras. Digital cameras are ideal as you can instantly see the picture you have just taken, whereas I had my trusty 35mm camera and had to wait until I got my photos developed. We fully

Face in the window? Charleville Castle

investigated the location, carrying out both group and solo vigils in all the reported haunted locations of the castle. Alas, this night we were to be disappointed. At 6:30am we retired to bed but I could not sleep with excitement from the truly fascinating night I had just experienced. The following day as agreed we assisted Dudley in clearing shrubbery from around the grounds of the castle.

I have investigated the castle many times since this and have moved through the ranks of the Paranormal Research Association of Ireland. I am now their security advisor and part of their core group. This means I investigate all locations the group are requested to investigate. Happily I have become quite busy with most of my work coming from the private sector. I find these investigations more interesting than large stately building investigations because I am helping people with deep emotional concerns of being terrorised in their own homes by ghosts, spirits or poltergeist activity. However the challenge of an investigation in a large location is equally as exciting.

However there is an absence of reference books to help the budding ghost hunter find locations to investigate in Ireland. This was my inspiration for writing this book. I will guide you through every aspect of investigating a reported haunted location including encounters with ghosts, spirits or poltergeists and detailed information on how to communicate with the other world and what methods you should use.

I have also included a list of reported haunted locations in Ireland with some personal stories from Irish people who have encountered ghosts.

What Haunts Ireland?

From her northern-most point to her southern shores Ireland is filled with the legends of haunting, demons and death warnings that will rival the legendary Transylvania and the tale of Dracula written by an Irish man, Bram Stoker. From the stateliest mansion to a castle ruin there are stories of ghosts, the Banshee and the Headless Horseman. The most common statement by any witness to these events is, 'I saw a ghost', but what exactly do they mean by this? And what are all the other ghosts, sprits, residual energy, grounded spirits, visitation ghosts or spirits, crisis ghosts, anniversary spirits, ghosts that walk through walls, poltergeists and banshee that haunt Ireland all about? If you look up the dictionary under the heading of 'ghost' you get a very simple definition: *an apparition of a dead person that is believed to appear to the living.* As I started my journey into the paranormal world I believed just that, a ghost is a ghost. But I quickly realised that this world goes far deeper than I originally thought and that there is in fact a whole spectrum of spirits that come under the simple heading of "Ghost". To simplify this complex gathering of spirits I have broken them up into their respective headings so that each one will present itself in a clear and simple way for you to understand.

Residual energy is what we experience when we say ghost. It is a playback of a past event. The apparition was once living but has left an impression in time within a building. Such apparitions are recordings of an event captured by the structure of the building. There are numerous theories as to how these residual hauntings have come to be. The main one is that they are like a video playback. Video and audiotapes capture sounds and images on a film using a special material that is oxidized. Certain building materials, such as slate and stone and some iron nails used in many older buildings have been found to have a similar oxidized material in them, thus making it somewhat possible for the building to record events in its structure. The materials store the energy created by these joyful or traumatic events and play them back at a later time. We are not sure what triggers the playback, sometimes it can be as simple as construction work or renovations being carried out on the location. Remember that these ghostly apparitions are only a playback; they are not spirits and cannot see you, interact with you or harm you in any way. This type of haunting is the most common type encountered in Ireland. Once a residual energy event is triggered it is more than likely to keep on replaying. This could be nightly, monthly or yearly depending on how traumatic the event was. As there cannot be any interaction it is impossible for mediums to cleanse a building of this type of haunting.

Grounded spirits are spirits stuck within the confines of a building or place. They either do not know how to cross over to the higher plain or simply do not want to. They will continue to haunt the location to which they most feel attached but like all spirits can move about freely and at will. I have several theories as to why spirits are grounded. One is that they simply do not know how to cross over to the light. These spirits are a little more complicated and more interesting than any other residual energy. When you step into the atmosphere of a grounded spirit not only do you look upon it, it can look back at you and acknowledge you in its atmosphere. The first time I experienced this I could feel the hairs along the back of my neck standing on end and my heart pounded in my chest. This is when you realise that you are not alone in this world. These types of spirits are what I call the Holy Grail of paranormal activity. For a paranormal investigator to stumble upon they are a joy to witness. Should you find that you have a grounded spirit on your property and do not like the thought of sharing your space with them, a good medium will be able to assist any spirit who wishes to cross over to do so with ease.

The following story told to me by a friend is a classic case of a grounded spirit haunting a location and in need of some help in crossing over.

"When I moved into a brand new house I looked forward to making it our home. But after living in

the house for a few months I noticed a shadow moving across some of the rooms every now and then. I put it down to my imagination. This continued for a while and objects would disappear and turn up some time later. Then one afternoon while cooking lunch I looked out the back door to see a monk dressed in a coarse gown gathered together with a rope belt. His face wore a frightened expression. He stood in the middle of the garden looking back at me.

Some months later I was watching television. My husband was at work and the children were in bed. The room appeared foggy but I put it down to my tiredness. However I had the same experience some nights later. Another night the dog started to chase something around the room stopping finally facing the corner ready to attack whatever he could see. I left the room and went to bed wondering what was happening in my home. I could sense it was something to do with the monk I had seen in the garden. As time went on I could feel the room becoming icy cold when in fact it was warm out side. I could also feel that whatever was happening wasn't pleasant. This continued for about a year and I eventually welcomed a visit from my dad's partner who is psychic. She confirmed that I had not been imagining these events and that the presence I was sensing was my great grandmother who was or is still watching over me and protecting me. The monk on the other hand was a different story. She sensed evil about him. We went into the sitting room. This was the room in *which most of the occurrences had happened. She took my crystal necklace which I had been wearing and held it beside a bottle. She asked the presence to tap the bottle to let us know how long it had been here. It started to bang on the side of the bottle eight times, signifying eight hundred years. There is an old pathway that runs through my house and she sensed spirits still travel it. My research found that the monk had once travelled this path from the sea back to his monastery. On his return he had killed the pregnant mother of his baby in the church, now my home. We sent the child through the light so that she could rest at last and also banished the monk from entering my house. I felt my faith in God helped me through, as this monk was evil. Things still disappear and then turn up, but that is just my little friend so I don't mind. The monk eventually went through the light and I could sense peace at last."*

Others spirits may not know they are deceased; their lives might have ended so suddenly that as far as they are concerned they are still living and are most likely still searching for their loved ones. Sadly they have probably already passed over to the spirit world on a higher plain. Sometimes these spirits can become angry and troublesome, especially if they return to their houses and cannot understand why they are being ignored. But there are also grounded spirits who have had such a joyous connection with either a place or people that they simply do not want to cross over and are happy to be grounded.

Visitation spirits: Spirits that come in visitation can easily be mistaken for grounded spirits as they, like grounded spirits, will interact with you when you enter their atmosphere. These spirits have crossed over and gone through their healing process.

For some reason they have decided to return to either visit their loved ones or a favourite place frequented when they were living and earth bound. They can also come back to protect or reassure loved ones when they are in danger or in need of comforting. But there is one thing you must remember and this will become apparent when researching your location. If a spirit was a kind-hearted person while earth bound, that personality will carry over with them and make them a happy, kind, loving spirit. Equally if they were a nasty person, for example a violent person while earth bound that personality will also carry over with them into the spirit world. We are who we are and when we die we leave our bodies behind. Our souls and our personalities remain with us in the after life. So if during your research into a location you find it had a violent past be on your guard and expect to encounter a violent spirit. There is a method of spiritual protection that you can use before entering any location. You can find this in the section on "Developing your psychic abilities" later on in the book. I would recommend that you enlist the use of a good medium to join you on your investigations as he or she will be able to tell you if you are dealing with a grounded spirit or a spirit in visitation and even more importantly if it's a kind spirit or nasty one. If you cannot enlist the services of a medium then rely on your sixth sense. Feel the energy that is building up and act accordingly.

Death-bed/near-death apparitions: Thousands of such incidents have been reported and investigated. One typical death-bed apparition is the vision by a dying person of their already deceased relative or relatives coming to collect them and bring them over to the next world. This usually happens just a few minutes before the person finally passes into the afterlife. These visions bring great comfort to the dying person and without question will make the passing over easier at this traumatic point in the spiritual cycle of a person.

Crisis spirits: A crisis spirit is the spirit of a loved one or friend that at the time of their death pays a visit to say that it will see you again in the next world. But it may also come to warn of grave danger. Crisis spirits may not always show themselves in a physical form, but may let you know that they are there by putting their favourite tune in your head or by putting their smell into your atmosphere. You are unlikely to encounter a crisis spirit on any investigation, but should you do so rest assured that it will be someone you know and love just popping by to say goodbye as they pass on, or to protect you should you be in grave danger.

Anniversary ghosts: As a paranormal investigator I often rely on luck combined with a lot of patience. Indeed I have sat in silence for long periods of time in cold damp locations.

Much of the personal evidence that I have gathered over the years is as a result of just sheer luck. All with the exception of what are known as "anniversary spirits" or ghosts. Anniversary ghosts or spirits are re-enactments by residual energy or spirits of people who only return on the anniversary of a momentous or tragic occasion in their lives. In the case of an *anniversary residual energy haunting* the event will be re-enacted and played over and over again. Unlike normal residual events anniversary spirits may return on the anniversary of an event in their earth lives and re-enact that event. And there may be some interaction between both the spirit and you, should you happen to walk into their energy while the re-enactment is taking place.

One classic case of an anniversary ghost is that of Olivia Lenox-Conyngham of Springhill House in Derry. One night in a fit of desperation her husband George Lenox-Conyngham shot himself. Olivia ran down the corridor of their home to stop him but she was too late. Since then several people who have stayed in the house claim to have seen an apparition of a woman running down the corridor and banging her hands on the door of the room where George shot himself and then vanishing into nothing.

Spirits are everywhere but why do they contact us without us initiating any contact with them? Simply because they want us to know that they are there passing through. Whatever method they use to let you know they are present be grateful for it, as they have put a lot of effort into making the crossing to be with you. Let them know that you love them. Say it out loud; they will hear it and will take that love with them. If you happen to be visiting a place and find that a spirit wants to let you know that they are there, look upon this as a blessing. You might experience incidents such as your clothing being pulled, you may sense a gentle blowing in you ear, or feel someone brushing against you. You might report the smell of cooking despite the fact that there is no cooking going on, or electrical items might switch themselves on and off while you are in a hotel room. Sometimes they pop over to protect you when your life is in danger.

One of the most beautiful stories of spirit contact was passed on to me by a work colleague. After her family lost their mother they all grieved for her but her death affected one of her sisters more than the rest of the family. A few months after her mother died Tara received a phone call from her sister Paula, who was very depressed. She explained that Paula had returned home and was sitting on the sofa still wearing her coat, which was wet from the heavy rain outside. She explained to her sister that she had been thinking of her mother and feeling very down when she noticed a snow white dove outside the patio doors. Paula thought this was strange as it was such a dull rainy day. She told Tara that she thought it was their mum trying to tell her something. Tara asked Paula to ask the dove to verify that it was her mum by flying over to the tree that she had planted in her garden. No sooner had she said this than the dove flew over to the tree and back to the doors. The sisters got their answer. Then Paula opened her patio door thinking the bird would fly away like all birds do. But it came into the house and walked around the dining room and sitting room. It stayed in the house long enough for Paula to take several pictures of it sitting just in front of her Christmas tree. The dove left as her feelings of depression lifted. For now, all the family know that their mum is OK and that she is still watching over them.

One question I am often asked as a paranormal investigator is 'why do ghosts and spirits walk through walls?' Well it's not because they are taking a short cut or just because they can. It is in fact because the property has been altered. Where once a door stood now a wall or a new property stands. Spirits walk or travel through a building or place in their time not ours even though we see them. They see the surroundings through their eyes as they were when they were living. If you can only see a spirit from the waist up your research may show that there are still the remains of a building underneath the present one.

I recall investigating a property not far from where I live. The owner claimed to have seen what he believed to be the spirit of a little boy about the same height as his own son. Exciting as this was to us as investigators we learned that the building had been altered. We discovered that the part of the building where he saw the apparition was a new extension onto the old building that he had built himself. Stepping outside to survey the building we observed that there were three deep steps leading up to the newly constructed front door. This new extension had been built in the old garden of the property and the old path was where he had witnessed the spirit. This path was now part of the new concrete flooring. Armed with this new information we used his son's height as reference and placed an adult out in the new garden, three steps lower than the inside of the building. What the man had seen was not a little boy but a fully-grown man passing along the original pathway. He also reported other noises that coincidently only started after the building work commenced. This residual energy had been triggered by building work. We told the owner that this apparition could be a regular visitor to his house and because it was more than likely residual energy it would be almost impossible to clear the property.

Poltergeist: Hollywood has fuelled our imagination with weird and strange demons that enter our world through our televisions and take our children into another realm. But just what are poltergeists? A poltergeist is a malevolent, mischievous form of energy that manifests itself in a number of ways. Strange noises, the movement or disappearance of objects, and strong abnormal odours are but a few examples. The word poltergeist is a German word meaning literally "noisy spirit." Why exactly poltergeist activity occurs has been the subject of great debate by experts and scientists for decades. Independent studies carried out on poltergeist activity have shown that the majority of cases involve an individual and not the property itself. The phenomenon seems to be linked to a type of subconscious psycho kinesis (PK) on the part of the individual. Poltergeist activity usually begins and ends abruptly. An individual incident can last for several hours or several years stopping and returning during this time. Poltergeist activity can also be associated with supernatural forces including demonic influences brought about by foolish dabbling in the occult and untrained participation in Ouija boards. There are some aspects of their activity however that make them different and it is worth becoming familiar with them. Poltergeists are not spirits at all but they are a build up of PK energy that a living person is unknowingly controlling. Poltergeist activity can be triggered by a living person's state of mind in any location, at any time. However it builds-up over time to a climax with a sudden stop, then the energy must build up again and the activity will start all over again. Poltergeists can travel anywhere with any one individual.

Another subject of great debate within the paranormal world is why ghosts and spirits appear fully dressed when we witness them and how clothes can be deemed haunted. There should be in principle no reason for ghosts to wear clothes at all, whereas we require clothing to keep us warm in winter and cool in summer. Clothes are also an extension to our personality and help us to conform to social requirements. Ghosts always seem to reflect in their clothing the period of dress that is associated with them when they lived. One theory behind the subject of why ghosts are dressed is that they are wearing the clothing in which they died or were laid to rest.

Animal connections: Ghosts are associated with animals in two ways. Some animal spirits manifest themselves while other animals can see ghosts. The ghosts of animals are as common as ghosts themselves. Hundreds of accounts of the ghostly presence of animals have been documented through time. When one Dublin gentleman died the grief at the loss of his master was too much for his dog and he refused to leave his graveside at Glasnevin cemetery in Dublin. The Newfoundland hound slowly starved to death. Eyewitnesses have often reported seeing a ghostly hound beside the old man's grave. As with human hauntings different types of spirit animals have both residual and visitation haunting.

Because animals are more sensitive than humans and hear and see things on a different wavelength to us, it is believed that they also see and hear spirits and ghosts before we do. If you take the time to watch your dog's behaviour you will notice that he or she will know when a member of your family is returning home before they even come down the road. They will be waiting at the door or window barking and wagging their tail waiting for them to round the corner. How do they know? How do they know the difference between strangers walking up the path at night and someone they know? And when a spirit enters the atmosphere you will suddenly notice your dog standing still, apparently staring at nothing. He might seem to follow it around the room as it moves or he may even bark loudly in the direction he sees the spirit. We just have to accept the fact that animals are superior to us when it comes to sensing the presence of spirits and they make a useful tool on any investigation.

21

Irish Legends and
Death Warnings

The Banshee
The Banshee is a woman appointed to warn families of
the imminent death of one or more of its members. Legend
has it that she can only appear and cry for one of the five
families by the names of O'Neil, O'Brien, O'Connor,
O'Grady and Kavanagh. Having said that, with inter-family
marriages through time this might be extended to just about
anyone. The banshee comes in several forms but the most
common is that of an elderly woman who sits outside the
house of the chosen family. It is here that she will wail. She
has very often been reported to dress in a grey cloak and is
always combing her long white hair as she cries her
shrieking wail. She can cry for several nights outside a house
waiting for a family member to die. As a young child my
mother would often warn me to watch out for the banshee.
If she looked at you she would throw her comb at you and
if it hit you it would mark you forever or she could take you

away. I recall several late nights when I would run home in fear of seeing the banshee. I have often mistaken the wailing cry of a cat to that of the crying banshee and would run as if my life depended on it. In my time as a paranormal investigator I have heard hundreds of stories about her but I have never seen her. This is not to say she does not exist. So remember if you should hear her crying you are safe for it's only the person that she is calling for that cannot hear her death cry.

Death Coach

Death is the driver of the "death coach" or as he is otherwise known the Coach-a-bower. In many parts of Ireland, it is believed that Death had to venture into the land of the living to retrieve souls. Hence, the personification of the death coach, a black plumed funeral coach pulled by huge black horses and driven by a headless coachman. Others say the Banshee herself drives it, but regardless of who drives the death coach it is feared because it is in effect Death approaching. Even today many old people fear the sound of hooves coming down the road and hope that the horse will not stop in front of their home. It is believed that if the death coach stops to claim a soul the driver dismounts and knocks three times on the door signalling that someone in that house has just died.

Death Comes Knocking

When the Angel of Death knocks at a door it is a sign that she has arrived to collect a soul. There have been many recorded accounts of knocking on a door and yet when the door was opened there was nobody there. Then the knocking would be heard at the back door and likewise nobody there. For those who heard the knocking the message was clear. The Angel of Death had just paid a visit and a loved one was now deceased. I heard such knocking on our door when I was a child. There were three loud knocks on the front door. When my father answered no one was there. Then there were three loud knocks on the back door. At this point we all ran out into the yard but like before, nobody was there. Later that night my mother heard the sad news of the death of her mother. I will never forget that night. Folklore had become harsh reality.

Ghost Hunting and
Investigating a Location

As a nation we are fascinated with being scared out of our wits. People just love being in scary situations either watching a scary movie or riding a wild rollercoaster. We are addicted to the fear factor. The paranormal world is no exception to this and we all love a good ghost story. Some of us like to take this one stage further and actually go out and search for ghosts. Ghost hunting and paranormal investigation is a fascinating and rewarding hobby. Before you rush into this world there is one golden rule of ghost hunting that you must never break and that is, never ever go out on your own; there must always be a minimum of two people on any one location.

Let's look at what is involved in ghost hunting. The first thing you must remember is that unless you have been invited by the owners of a building you cannot simply go to a building and investigate it, even if it is deserted. Someone somewhere owns it or is the trustee of the

27

property. If it is deserted then look up the land registry files or consult with the local county council or corporation. Once you have found the owner or trustee make contact with them. Having secured an invite to investigate a location the hard work now begins. You must gain a full history and background check on the location. This must include names of previous owners. Were there any tragic deaths or happenings there? Was the present building built over a previous structure that was pulled down or attacked at one time? Investigate any stories or folklore about the building. Check to see if anyone living in the building sleepwalks. I know this might seem like a silly question but if they sleepwalk they might move objects around while doing so. They could move pictures around or lay them flat on a shelf only to wake in the morning and wonder what the hell is going on.

Remember you have to rule out all the obvious. Listen carefully to the story you are being told about the haunting, make good notes and use your tape recorder. Talk to other members of the family especially young children (with their parents present); they are a world of knowledge. *I remember once being on an investigation in a private home. From what the parent was telling us it sounded like it was the spirit of her late husband. After we spent some time chatting to her youngest daughter the picture became clear. She told us that her babysitter played strange board games with her friends while babysitting. As she described the board it soon became apparent that it was an Ouija board. She also told us that the babysitter would make drawings on the kitchen floor in salt of a large circle with a star in the middle of it. What was described to me was a Pentagram, the five-pointed star circled. The theory behind this is that while you are sitting or standing inside the pentagram reciting a ritual prayer you are protected from whatever you call over from the spirit world. The babysitter was stupidly and dangerously dabbling in the occult.*

Make a sketch of the building and copy it for every member of the team in case anyone gets lost or separated. Make regular notes on your map as to the locations of reported happenings. Having gathered all your information you can now schedule your night's investigation. On the night of the investigation discuss with the owners exactly how you will be investigating their location, particularly if they live in the house. There are two schools of thought on investigating a location, the scientific and the spiritual. There is an array of equipment available to the paranormal investigator. Some of these items may sound obvious or a little strange, but if you do not record or capture an image of a paranormal happening then your story will only be added to the thousands of wild stories told around fires at night.

The most basic piece of equipment is a torch. Now this might sound a little obvious, but as most investigations are carried out at night a good flashlight could be your only friend in the cold lonely dark room of a castle; especially if you start to hear strange noises around you. And of course always bring spare batteries. A torch with a red filter glass attached is especially useful as the red glow it

A good torch may
be your best friend.

gives off will not interfere with your natural night vision.
Bring some night light candles with you so that you can
find your way back to your base room to the other
members of the team should you lose your torch.

Cameras and Camcorders

It is said that orbs and spirits can only be caught on camera
using digital cameras. This is not altogether true as I have
caught a red glow hovering in front of me using a 35mm
single lens reflex cameras. The 35mm camera should be a
good quality SLR using a fast film of no slower than 800
speed. Digital cameras should have a minimum of three
million pixels and a card of at least 256mb. This will allow
you to take pictures on superfine settings. I also use a
digital camcorder with night vision which allows me to
record in total darkness and you can move around in the
dark using the small screen on the side of the camcorder to
see where you are going. They are also useful for recording
orbs and for placing over a trigger object if you are using
one. A tripod will also come in very handy; in a cold castle
in the middle of the night taking a steady shot with cold
hands can be quite difficult.

Thermometer

I would recommend using two types of thermometer, both digital for ease of reading. An ambient thermometer will give you the ambient room temperature while a second non-contact thermometer will give you an accurate reading from any surface you point it at. You can detect a cold spot and follow the cold spot around the room using one of these types.

EMF (Electro Magnetic Field) Detector

An EMF detector measures the electro magnetic field given off by any electronic device. These will include mobile phones, microwave cookers, televisions, power lines; anything in fact that has a power source. Spirits use energy to travel and manifest into either spirit lights, 'orbs' or full manifestations. When using an EMF detector certain points should be taken into account. Firstly, make note of the location of all electronic devices in the building you are investigating. Take a reading of the electro magnetic field around the device and write it down in your notes. This is part of what we call a base line investigation. Now that you have all your EMF readings jotted down, any reading above 2.5 mill gauss could predict the presence of a spirit within close proximity to the EMF detector.

I recall investigating a private house in Dublin. The house had what is commonly called poltergeist activity. Their 14-year-old son's bedroom was the main hive of activity. I took all the readings using the EMF detector and thermometer. I placed the EMF detector and ambient thermometer on his bed and sat patiently on a lone vigil. I was there no less than 45 minutes when the room temperature dropped. My breath was vaporising and the EMF detector started spiking. I got a 4.8 mill gauss reading on the EMF and a 12 degree drop in ambient room temperature. This lasted for approximately two to three minutes then the spiking stopped and the room temperature returned to normal. At the end of your investigation load all your readings into your computer and transfer onto a graph that will show you what happened during the investigation.

Tape recorder, EMF (Electro Magnetic Field) detector
and thermometer

Tape Recorder

A tape recorder is a valuable tool on location. In your initial investigation phase it can be used to record an interview with the owner of the location, making your pre-investigation notes easier to work on. The main purpose of the tape recorder is for Electronic Voice Phenomena or

EVP. EVP is the practice of attempting to record spirits or ghosts using recording devices. The sounds that are recorded on tape in the background are sonic events of unknown origin which can sometimes be heard on electronic devices. The best way of conducting an EVP experiment is to press record and just speak normally asking questions like 'is there any spirit person here who would like to communicate with me?'. Stay quiet for a few seconds then repeat. If you know the name of the suspected ghost or spirit then call them by name, asking the same question. Once you have done this several times, replay and see what you have recorded. You might just be surprised with your findings. Other reported EVP have been ghostly voices heard as background noise over a radio station

Some other items that you may find helpful are: Stud Detector, a builder's tool that detects electronic cable and plumbing pipes behind walls. This could save hours of good hunting time. Point-to-Point Laser Alarms, small battery-operated alarm devices used to protect an entrance

Stud detector

where there is no mains supply. I like to use this alarm device on a staircase where there are reports of footsteps. Place the alarms facing each other and activate the laser beam. Anything that breaks the

Point-to-Point laser alarms

beam will sound the alarm. Passive Infrared Alarm; this alarm sends a passive infra-red beam across the room and should a door or window be opened the alarm will activate.

Trigger Objects

This is the only positive and truly reliable way to discover paranormal activity.

A trigger object can be anything you like it to be. It can be something originally from the building or something you brought to the location. All that is required is that it must be capable of being laid flat on a white sheet of paper. After you have laid it down carefully draw an outline around it with either a pencil or biro taking care not to move the object. Leave a 'locked off' camcorder (a camcorder

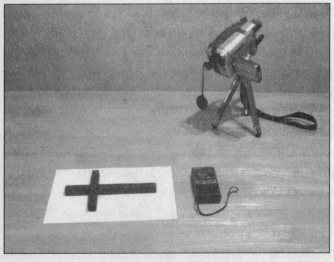

Classic trigger objects

34

left on its own in a room) recording the object. Please make sure that all of the paper is in shot. Lock the room or use one of your alarms to guard the room. If, when you return any of the trigger objects have been moved and the evidence is on tape, and you are sure that the room was not entered by another member of the team or occupier of the property, then you have first class evidence of paranormal activity.

Pre-investigation

A pre-investigation meeting is essential to lay down the rules of the investigation. If you are investigating an occupied location note out of bounds areas. These are usually the owner or proprietor's private quarters. If it is a deserted or derelict building take note of all areas of danger and stay clear of them.

I always take some private time before an investigation. Often I say a private prayer and though I am not religious I find it works for me. *The Lord is my shepherd, I shall not want; He makes me lie down in green pastures. He leads me beside still waters; He restores my soul. He leads me in paths of righteousness for His name's sake. Even though I walk through the valley of the shadow of death, I fear no evil; for Thou art with me. Thy rod and thy staff, they comfort me. Thou preparest a table before me in the presence of my enemies; Thou anoint my head with oil, my cup overflows. Surely goodness and mercy shall follow me all the days of my life; and I shall dwell in the house of The Lord forever.* While saying this prayer I like to imagine the brightest pure purple light entering my body through the top of my head and flowing through my body.

Then wrapping the light around me I know it will protect me from any evil I may come upon. I also like to send this light home to my loved ones to protect them from harm while I am away and of course to the rest of the team as they set out on the night's adventure. Don't forget as you set off on your investigation to talk to the spirits; they might just answer you. Use your tape recorder as you do this. Talk in a calm voice. I suggest the following: '*Are there any spirits here that would like to show themselves? If so please show yourself either by making a noise, touching one of the group or appearing in either light form or showing yourself*'. Always be respectful towards spirits, they might be more inclined to show themselves. '*We are here with the greatest of respect and we mean you no harm. We only want to make contact with you. Please help us by showing yourself.*'

When investigating a location fright can be infectious. Try to remain calm even if you are scared. The dead cannot harm you; they don't possess enough energy to do this. Demons and other such energy sources from the darkest realms can, but you are unlikely to encounter these in any of your investigations. Your first encounters may be fearful but you will become more confident with time.

If during an investigation you are fortunate enough to have some sort of interaction from the spirit world, thank them for the huge effort they have just made to contact you. They will have had to gather a lot of energy to do so. Be active and enthusiastic; if you just sit doing nothing you will have a boring uneventful night. Put some effort into it and you will be rewarded.

Orbs or spirit lights

These are reported to be the first manifestation of spirits but I am sceptical of their authenticity. If you get an old dusty rug and jump on it in the dark while someone takes a picture of you using flash photography, you will see thousands of orbs in the picture. What would be significant would be an orb captured on camcorder reacting to your commands. For example if it moves up after you requested it to do so or down to a similar command. Then you have interaction with an intelligent source and not just a dust particle caught in the light of flash photography.

Spot the orb hanging just above the well.

When morning comes the group should discuss their experiences. Before heading to bed you could leave a camcorder running 'locked off' in the room where you are sleeping perhaps. You might just catch a playful spirit popping out as you sleep. Before leaving the location report any activity to the owners.

We have looked at the scientific path to investigating a reported haunted location; now let's look at the spiritual approach. As with the scientific method you should carry out a background check of the location and interview all living there to get a clear picture of what you may be dealing with.

Unlike the scientific approach the spiritual methods have been in use for hundreds of years with some convincing and well-documented results, though some of these methods should not be practised without the guidance of a trained medium.

Ouija Board: One of the most common is the Ouija board which dates back to Pythagoras in 540BC and was reportedly used by both the Egyptians and the Chinese. The French spiritualist, M. Planchette invented the concept of the Ouija Board in 1853. The modern board that we recognise today is a wooden board with the numbers 1-0, the letters A-Z, Yes and No and Hello and Goodbye painted onto its surface. Elija J Bond and William Fuld of Baltimore invented this version of the board around 1892. The board is placed in the centre of a table or on the floor. A wedge or glass is placed in the centre of the board with your fingers placed lightly on top. The theory is that you call out for any spirit present to communicate with you. When the wedge or glass begins to move you have spirit communication. But you must trust everyone around the board. If and when you get a reaction ask the spirit to spell out its name. The wedge or glass should move to the letters spelling out its name and so forth, depending on the question.

I must stress that Ouija boards are dangerous and not to be trifled with.

You have no control over what kind of spirit comes across from the spirit world and a lot of nasty spirits mask themselves as nice spirits until you have brought them too far; then they reveal their true nastiness. With this in mind I would never recommend their use without a trained medium present. A medium can give the group protection and open up and close a reading correctly, ensuring no nasty spirits remain trapped here to wreak havoc later. I stress, however, that I would not recommend the use of ouiji boards.

Séance: A Séance is probably the most common method used by mediums and paranormal investigators investigating haunted locations in Ireland.

Séance is the French for "sitting" and means a sitting of a group of people for the purpose of communication with the spirit world. As with the Ouija board I recommend that a medium head the sitting. To conduct a séance a round table is advisable as it is more comfortable, but any table will do. If no table is available standing or sitting on the floor is fine. Sit around the table with a lighted candle placed in the middle. Place your hands palms down on the table lightly touching the hands of the person sitting beside you. Place your feet comfortably on the floor but not crossed as this can upset the flow of energy. Select one member of the group to head the séance. Clear your mind of all thoughts and feel the energy flow through your body in a clockwise direction. Focus on the candle in front of you. Whoever is heading the séance should now start communicating. Unlike the Ouija Board, during a séance you are likely to only make contact with the spirit or spirits who are connected with the building. You will get answers to direct questions concerning the building's history or the spirit itself. The information you get can be checked against the background information you learnt during your research into the building's history. You may also contact spirits directly connected with individuals around the table. They are spirit guides though some people call them angels. After you have gathered the information you require from the spirit world close the séance by thanking the spirits for their help and participation and asking them to return to the spirit world. This is a very important part of any séance and must be conducted by whoever is heading the séance.

Scrying: Another fascinating method used to make contact with the spirit world is scrying. Scrying can be done with a number of different surfaces which include water, placed in a dark bowl – or small pools, mirrors, crystal ball gazing, candles and the embers of a fire at night. All of these methods work, but you will probably find one that suits you most. Using a dimly lit room is the most common atmosphere for the practice of scrying. The method that I use is to sit in front of a large mirror tilted slightly against a wall. During my scrying session I gaze steadily into the scrying surface and allow my point of focus to wander a bit. Eventually, I will be able to pick out shapes or images in the scrying surface. These may appear as crude sketches, or occasionally with the clarity of a photograph. These images will appear behind you. Once this happens, images may begin to form in your mind, no longer projected onto the scrying surface. Allow your attention to focus on these mental images. From this point forward the scrying surface is irrelevant. With time and practice you can look upon a whole new world. If you practice meditation it will be much easier. When you ask a question place a lot of energy into the answer as it will manifest faster for you. The amount of time you should dedicate to scrying can vary from a few minutes to a half hour.

Let's look at all the methods of this fascinating world a little deeper.

Mirror: Sitting in a darkened room with a candle placed between you and a mirror, gaze into the mirror. Do not focus on your reflection. After a while you may see yourself in past lives. The images will change. Watch the way your face changes; you may look younger or older or you may even grow facial hair. If you look to the side you may see the room change. You might find yourself looking at an old Victorian room with the images of spirit people going about their daily life.

Water: When scrying with water the bowl must be black or painted black. You can add black India ink to the water to turn it black. Place the bowl on a table in front of you. Close your eyes and concentrate on your breathing. Feel your breath fill your lungs and leave your body. Do this for a few minutes. Allow your mind and body to be relaxed and ready to see with more than the normal senses. Open your eyes and gaze down into the bowl at the dark water. Ask a question in your mind and wait for an answer. You may also just gaze into the bowl and watch for random images. They will appear perhaps as shadows at first but they will be there. You could also place a dish of water in a darkened room, light two candles and place them each side of the dish and follow the above instructions.

Crystal Ball: This may sound a bit "Gypsy Rose Lee" but this is the method used by mediums who use a crystal ball in their readings. Find a quiet place to begin scrying with a crystal ball. Clear your mind so that you can hear your thoughts without distractions and concentrate on the objects you see. Place the ball on a dark surface. Hold the ball between you hands. Looking deep into the crystal ball allow your eyes to focus on the images that may appear within the ball. Listen to your thoughts and they will guide you in the right direction. Images may move around within the ball and you can move the ball to view different images that appear within it.

Table Tipping: This originated in the parlour rooms of early Victorian times. This closely followed the ghost story that started on 31st March, 1848, in the town of Arcadia, New York. Two sisters, then 12 and 15, began communicating with the spirit world through raps and knocks on tables. Though people would later make claims of deception, Kate and Margaret Fox effectively began the craze for spiritualism that swept across America and Europe. With the growth in interest in communicating with the dead, developing methods and tools to facilitate these communications evolved as a matter of course. Table tipping was one such early method, where a group of people, usually led by a medium, would sit around a suitable table with their fingers resting on it and attempt to make contact with a spirit. If successful, the table would tip and knock on the floor, answering questions and even spelling out messages using a code of knocks for each letter of the alphabet. This was a long and tiring process. If you wish to try this place a bell that is suspended from underneath the table by a piece of string as this will give you a good indication of any movement in the table. The table must be on a flat surface and the table legs secure. Those participating should either sit or stand around the table with their hands lightly touching the edge of the table. As with Ouija and séance there is usually a spokesperson. This person will call out to the spirits present to make communication with them by moving or knocking the table. You must have faith in every person at the table as it can easily be moved by one person trying to fool the rest.

Automatic Handwriting: To practice automatic hand-writing you will need some large sheets of paper and a pen or a pencil. Sit on a comfortable chair at a table and place the paper flat on the table. Place your hand lightly on the paper holding the pen lightly too. Relax and concentrate on your breathing. Feel it flowing into your lungs and out again. Clear your mind of all conscious thoughts. Let the pen move freely across the paper but never direct it, as this will only give you a false reading. The point of this exercise is to receive information from the spirit world and not from your conscious thoughts. Do not be discouraged at first if nothing happens as the more you practice the better you will become at it. Even if you get information that seems irrelevant keep it. You might be surprised later on in your investigation.

Crystals and Dowsing Rods. For more than 7000 years dowsing rods and crystals have helped people to find water sources or lay lines. People use them by allowing energy flow through their body into their hands resulting in either the rods crossing or the crystal pendulum swinging or rotating as it's suspended from a string or light chain. The theory behind this is that when the energy level builds up, because of spirit activity near the user of the rods or crystal pendulums, that this energy is channelled through them causing the rods or pendulum to react. I have only ever been present once when a crystal pendulum was being used. It was by a young chap who joined us on one of our adventures to Charleville Castle, Co. Offaly. He claimed that he was in fact a white wizard and informed us that he was going to take on the black demon. What black demon? I was fascinated by this as there are no black demons in Charleville Castle. The wizard proclaimed that the black demon was in the dungeon area of the castle so off we went into the dungeon to see this white wizard take on the black demon. We all gathered around him as he produced from his pocket a crystal suspended from a gold chain. 'Can I have all lights off please?' he requested. With that there was total darkness. A few minutes later the white wizard proclaimed that the black demon was with us and that the crystal was spinning in his hand. All I could feel 'with us' was the castle's resident dog. I became intrigued with the antics of this wizard and pulled from my pocket a night vision scope that I had borrowed from one of the team members. Using the night scope I found the white wizard and to my amazement he was spinning the crystal himself. I protested and silence came over the dungeon followed by giggles from the rest of the team. Undeterred by this he continued with his show. During the rest of the night's investigation he claimed to be possessed by the demon no less than five times. Needless to say we never invited the great white wizard back to take part in any further investigation.

Tarot Cards and Angel Cards: Although reading tarot and Angel cards are not a method of making direct contact with the spirit world they are a means of getting messages from the spirit world. The spirits intervene in what cards you choose in direct response to the question asked by you. The use of both tarot and angel cards have long been associated with the paranormal world here in Ireland. The earliest reported use of tarot cards dates back to the fifteenth century. The oldest surviving tarot cards can be traced back to Northern Italy in 1440. These cards were hand-painted and originally used for a game called 'The Game of Triumphs'. This game was very popular with nobles of the time and quickly spread throughout Europe. While the designs of the cards have changed over the years their meanings remain the same. The only noticeable change has been the redesigning of the cards by makers to reflect the cultures of the various countries in which they are used. There are many different forms of deck but the fundamental process of reading cards remains the same. I will just give a brief explanation on tarot cards. The original deck of 78 tarot cards were divided into 4 suits of 14 cards, the standard ace to 10, page, knight, queen and king along with 22 unnumbered trumps. Over the years the trumps were re-numbered 1 to 21 with the Fool remaining unnumbered or considered zero.

The Tarot deck consists of the Major and Minor Arcana.

Major Arcana

The Fool infinity of the circle indicates that a person has not yet reached his/her potential.

The Magician focuses on an idea and brings it to life.

The High Priestess is the link between the conscious and subconscious mind.

The Emperor is older and wiser than the Magician. It

rules the conscious elements in the material world.

The Empress card indicates the creativity and imagination that brings forth the manifestation of things. The stars on her crown represent the twelve zodiac signs that indicate time and bring desire to fruition. The Hierophant represents our inner self, the teacher, and intuition. He collects the facts based on reason.

The Lovers card symbolizes relationships and partners. A union of opposites indicates that we must follow a path to understanding by using our conscious, subconscious and super-conscious minds.

The Chariot card is symbolic of the soul and the physical shell that controls the positive and negative forces.

The Strength card represents the power of control over material forces.

The Hermit has reached a place where he has mastered all elements of the past.

Wheel of Fortune represents the grasp on the persona by understanding who you really are.

Justice rules the laws of cause and effect by correcting the wrongs of the past.

The Hanged Man represents a change of view signifying that everything is not as it seems.

Death represents transformation or rebirth.

Temperance is a blend of positive and negative that provides a balance between the conscious and the subconscious mind.

The Devil represents blindness and misconception. It is a wasting of energy or denial.

The Tower symbolizes abrupt understanding.

The Star gathers knowledge from the pools of the conscious and the subconscious mind.

The Moon represents the evolution of spirit that slowly begins to learn and focus more clearly.

The Sun is the giver of life. It is a neutral card that teaches us to understand that love for all things must be achieved without bias.

Judgment represents a healthy mind and spirit that has acquired a better understanding of everything spiritual.

Finally the **World** represents a never-ending cycle of life that remains unchanged and orderly.

Within the Minor Arcana cards are:

The Suit of Wands, the realm of spirit that represents ideas as the primary or original thought.

The Suit of Cups, the realm of mental manifestation of ideas.

The Suit of Swords, the realm of astral swords representing action of thought.

The Suit of Pentacles, the Realm of the physical or material.

Angel Cards: The Angel Oracle was created from forty of the angel paintings of Sulamith Wulfing. Wulfing was born in Germany in 1901 and had her first art exhibition at twenty-two going on to exhibit much of her fantasy and fairy tale art throughout her long life. She died in 1988. Wulfing called angels her "consolers, leaders, companions and guards". Each card in the Angel Oracle shows one of Wulfing's angels in colour on one side, and again in smaller, black-and-white versions on the other side. Under these small reproductions are keyword meanings and an inspirational message that goes with it. There is no instruction booklet for the Angel Oracle. The cards are supposed to be used for meditation and daily guidance. They say that Angels have the power to touch every one of us with their protection, guidance and eternal love. With the Angel Oracle you know you have the means to access this divine wisdom. The beautifully illustrated angel cards, one for each of the angels in the heavenly realm, will offer you or others clarity of thought and insight into your innermost feelings.

Holding the cards in your left hand, make a fist with your right hand and knock on the deck three times. Open your hand as if you were discarding rubbish from it. This is to clear the deck of any energy from a previous reading. Hold the cards close to your heart and fan them out touching each card as you do so. At this point you will ask the angels to help and guide you in your reading and understanding of the cards. Then shuffle the cards. If you are making a reading for yourself you will ask your question at this point. If you are reading for another person you will ask their question now too. A number will come into your head. This will be the number of cards you will take from the top of the deck when you have finished shuffling the deck.

Now lay the chosen cards face up from left to right. Your answer lies within. Cross reference the card against its meaning in the booklet and your angels will have given you the help and guidance you requested.

White Noise: White noise is a relative newcomer to the paranormal world. It involves the use of radios or televisions that are tuned into a non-station where you can hear only static on the radio or see white haze on the television accompanied by static sound. White noise can be used during a séance or table tipping. The theory behind white noise is that spirits can communicate through the wavelengths of the radio or television being used and you can hear them speak to you through the static noise. Some people have reported that they have heard their loved ones trying to communicate with them through their radios. They have even received messages from the spirit world through the use of white noise. I have been present on many occasions when white noise has been used but on those occasions nothing happened. That does not mean that white noise does not work as I have always said paranormal investigation is not an exact science.

Mediums and Psychics

Mediums or Psychics are for me like doctors. They all practice the same profession but seem to give a different diagnosis. However I recommend their use for several reasons. They give you insight into the spirits who either reside there or visit the location; they can also protect you from any nasty spirits or poltergeist activity that might be residing at a location.

Do take care in recruiting your medium. Make some background checks and ask for references. If they are genuine they will be glad to do this for you.

Developing your psychic abilities

Psychic ability is not a special gift only given to the chosen few. We all have the potential to develop the senses that we were born with. When we are young we all have this gift but as time goes by we suppress it until it becomes what we call our sixth sense. To unlock your powers you can embark on a journey that will change your life for the good. This is generally known as medium-ship. A medium is an individual who has the ability to receive or channel messages from the spirit world or other discorporate entities. There are mental mediums and psychic mediums. A mental medium will meditate focusing his mind on what is called the Alpha State of consciousness. While he or she is in the Alpha State they are fully awake and aware of what is happening around them and can move freely. Within this discipline there are five forms of medium-ship:

Clairvoyance: Clairvoyance is the psychic ability to see objects and visions or to gain information regardless of the distance. These visions may relate to the past or future. You can only see this vision in your mind's eye.

Clairaudience: Clairaudience is the receipt of messages in thought form from a spirit that exists in another realm. You 'hear' what they are saying in your mind. Only you can hear.

Clairsentience: Clairsentience is the ability to feel what has happened or what is about to happen without the experience of seeing or hearing it. It is an ability traditionally known as intuition or "gut feeling", your sixth sense.

Clairalience: Clairalience is the ability to experience distinct smells that others may not experience within the room. This can be connected to an event such as a fire that was in a building or the smell of cooking or of a favourite tobacco being smoked.

Clairambience: Clairambience is the ability to use the sense of taste to receive a message from the communicating spirit. This is commonly experienced in conjunction with Clairalience (smelling). All mediums have one of these talents, some have two or more, but to develop all five would be very rare indeed.

When a medium is conducting a reading or an investigation they can employ the following methods to allow the spirits to pass on messages or to communicate through them.

Trance: There are various degrees of trance. A trance occurs when a spirit either speaks through the medium or makes the medium reinact actions or bodily movements. In most cases the medium will remain conscious of what is being said through his/her vocal chords or to whatever movements he or she is making.

Automatic writing: Automatic writing is the process of writing from the subconscious. I have already discussed how to conduct automatic hand writing earlier in the book.

Psychometry: Psychometry is the ability to gather information from an object's history by handling it. The object acts as a link between the medium and spirit world. An alternative way of looking at it is that the object somehow records impressions from its owner and events in its history. As soon as the medium takes hold of the object he will get visions or other information belonging to its owner from the object.

Psychic Artists: Psychic artists are able to sketch or paint people in the spirit world who are then recognised by surviving family members or friends. Psychic artists can also give information about the subject drawn that they receive through either clairvoyance or clairaudience while conducting the sitting.

With all of the above the medium will have meditated and put his mind into the Alpha State. Psychic medium-ship on the other hand demonstrates the ability of spirit communication through the production of various psychic phenomena. Sadly this is a rare phenomenon. Psychic medium-ship was very common during Victorian times but has become a forgotten art. It can take more time and patience to practice. The conditions have to be just right for a spirit to manifest or appear in whatever form they choose to appear. As with mental communication, psychic communication has several different methods available for the practitioner to use. *Probably one of the most famous methods used by psychic mediums was that used by the famous British spiritualist medium Helen Duncan. To help support her six children and a disabled husband Helen Duncan travelled across Britain conducting séances. These were dramatic affairs in which ectoplasm reportedly oozed from her mouth and formed spirit manifestations, which spoke to the people gathered for the séance.* This ectoplasm is reported to be an energy matter taken from the medium's body. It is supposed to extrude from the medium through any opening but usually either through the nose or mouth. It is a seemingly life-like substance that is solid or vaporous in nature and can be transformed into visual limbs such as a face and even entire bodies of spirits. Ectoplasm is reported to have taken on several forms on many occasions. It can appear to be milky white in colour, visible or/and invisible. It is believed that if a spirit suddenly appears to a person with no medium present, the vision is made possible from ectoplasm drawn directly from the room.

Other methods used are as follows:

Transfiguration: A transfiguration medium has a mask-like form of ectoplasm covering or floating just in front of his/her face. This may take the form of the face of a spirit person that should be recognised by a family member present at a séance.

Levitation: Levitation is the movement of objects without normal means of support. This can be done by the use of psycho kinetic energy whereby objects would appear to float around a room during a séance.

Direct Voice: Direct Voice is a rare form of psychic phenomenon. It is the hearing of voices spoken during a séance. The Direct Voice is not the voice of the medium or of any of the sitters. The voices are heard from within the medium as if the medium were speaking for the spirit during a séance.

Independent Voice: Independent Voice communication occurs when voices are heard from the air.

Audible Phenomena: Audible phenomena are the most common forms of communication and include knocks, raps and taps heard during investigation. If you are successful in communicating with the spirit world through this form of communication, you should make the questioning of the spirits sufficiently simple for them to answer your questions. For example 'knock once for yes and twice for no'. It is the simplest form of communication with spirits and is often practised in conjunction with table tapping/tilting.

Many of these methods may sound daunting and off-putting but if this is your chosen path into the world of the paranormal I would recommend professional training.

So what is the key to unlocking this supernatural world of medium-ship that we all possess? The answer is through meditation. At the moment your mind is in what is called the Beta state and is processing vast amounts of information; noises from cars, trucks, people talking and information received through sight and smell. All are being processed at thirteen and thirty cycles per second. This is called the Beta Rhythm. In meditation you must relax, allowing brain rhythms of seven and thirteen cycles per second. This is called the Alpha State. Meditation is a state of mind that is relaxed yet alert. To achieve the desired state of mind you must relax. One of the most basic methods of meditating is to sit in a comfortable chair in a quiet warm room. Loosen any tight clothing and put on some soft background music. Breathe in and out listening to your breath as your lungs fill and empty. Focus on your breathing as you allow your body to relax. Do this for about five minutes. At this point you should be resting and taking deep regular breaths.

Now imagine your body heavier that it usually is. Starting at your feet, feel the weight lifting as you become lighter than air. Feel this sensation moving through your torso through your shoulders and arms and up through your head as the weight finally leaves you and dissipates into another dimension. Totally relaxed, but aware of your surroundings, you are now ready to move onto the next level.

At this point you must close your eyes and count the breaths you take in and out until you reach ten breaths. With your eyes closed imagine you have a third eye positioned inside your brain near the Pineal gland. The Pineal gland is about the size of a pea, and is in the centre of the brain in a tiny cave behind and above the Pituitary gland. This gland lies a little behind the root of the nose. It is located directly behind the eyes, attached to the third ventricle. When activated, the Pineal gland becomes your line of communication with the higher plane. The crown chakra reaches down until its vortex touches the Pineal gland. Now visualise an intense purple energy of light travelling through the energy centre in the head. With practice the vibration level of the astral body is raised. With your eyes closed imagine walking through a field of wheat. Feel your hands running across the tops of the wheat. Feel the breeze on your face and hear the sound of birds whistling. Now you will come to a pathway along a stream and you can see the water glistening in the sun as it gently flows along. You come to a bridge and now walk up to the bridge ignoring all outside noises remaining aware only of your senses as you approach the bridge. Look at the water running under the bridge and step onto it. Stop there, you do not need to cross the bridge, you are only there as an observer. Look across the bridge. What do you feel? What do you see? Look and observe whatever appears on the other side of the bridge. You are fully awake and all of your senses are alert even though you are totally relaxed. You are now in the Alpha State of mind.

Coming out of meditation correctly is equally as important as going into it. Slowly increase your breathing and open your eyes gently. Open and close your hands as you move your legs. As you begin to awaken from your meditation try to become aware of how you feel. Some people feel elated, others feel very emotional. These feelings are natural so allow them to happen as you are entering a new phase in your life. You have now left the state of meditation.

Before you begin to enter this next part of your development I would suggest that you bring a friend along as you may be distressed by what your third eye sees. Again choose a comfortable chair and loosen any tight clothing. As with meditation, focus on your breathing. Once you recognise that you have entered the Alpha State of meditation and are at the bridge, place your right hand on your forehead (or your left hand should you be left handed). Using your forefinger place it in the centre of your forehead between your eyes and rotate it in a clockwise direction. As you gently massage your forehead imagine a deep purple velvet curtain being lifted back. See it shine as it moves away. Now you see your third eye. See it open. It is the most beautiful eye you have ever seen. Look at it glisten with love. This is your eye and it will show you things that you have never seen before. Remember you are still only an observer. Do not cross the bridge but observe who or what appears on the other side for you. You have opened a powerful psychic channel and when you are finished it is very important to close it correctly. Watch it close. Imagine this purple light wrapping itself around you like a comfort blanket. Nothing can penetrate this shield of God's power. Now open your physical eyes and come out of the meditation as you normally would.

Conducting a candle rite: If you wish to protect yourself or your property from any kind of psychic or physical attack from evil spirits either in everyday life or during an investigation you should conduct a candle rite.

For this you will need four white candles, three green candles, a white sheet, a bowl of water and a bowl of salt. First place the white sheet on a table or other flat surface. Sprinkle a little water and salt over the sheet. Place the four white candles in a straight line approximately twelve inches apart. Place the three green candles in a straight line slightly in front of the white ones. They should be approximately six inches apart. Now sit in a high-backed chair facing the candles and light them. You should be no more than 24 inches from the row of green candles, seated in an upright position and facing them. Now repeat aloud the following prayer of invocation: *Dear God I pray that you will protect me from harm, from evil and from all thoughts of wickedness that may be directed against me or those that I love. Dear God I pray that you will wrap my body and the bodies of my family and all who live in this house in the protective cloak of your eternal love. Dear God please disperse the evil energy and thoughts that may have been directed against all those living within this house.* Repeat the above seven times, each time looking closely into the flames of the candles. You should now close with a prayer of your own choice or the following: *Dear God thank you for hearing my prayers. Please forgive those that would trespass against members of my family and me. Please bring peace and understanding to those who would spitefully use me. Allow me to live in the protection and love of your eternal light now and forevermore.*

Exorcists and Ghost Busters: When I tell people that I investigate haunted locations, ghosts and spirits they automatically think that I am a ghost buster. And I am often asked how to get rid of a ghost. People who have just moved into a house are rarely pleased to find out that it is haunted and that there are ghostly images about and noises keeping them awake at night. I surprise them by telling them that I am very happy to have ghosts and spirits around me and in my atmosphere.

There are people who specialise in the eviction of unwanted ghosts but check out their credibility before letting them inside your house and ask for references. You must make sure that the only house clearance they do is spiritual and not material.

Most ghost busters are psychic or employ the help of a psychic to clear the property. The process usually starts with the psychic opening up of communication with whoever is haunting your location. They will ask questions like 'Who are you?' 'How old are you?' 'Are you male or female?' The psychic will also ask if they know the owners of the property. This last question is an important one because you should find out if it is a malevolent ghost or not. In fact it may be just a deceased family member popping in to keep an eye on you. You might not want to get rid of it at all. But if you want your property cleared the process is quite simple. The psychic will make contact with whoever is haunting your location and establish dialogue with the spirit. If it is a spirit that does not know how to cross over or is afraid to cross over they will guide them towards the light. The light in this case is a vortex that links the earth world to the spirit world. As soon as the spirit reaches the vortex they will be greeted by a loved one who has previously been selected to greet them. They will guide the spirit into the spirit world. Should it be a malevolent spirit that refuses to leave your location the psychic can then call upon his own spirit guides to help him in clearing the property. Because his spirit guides are already in spirit life they can have a direct affect on the spirit haunting your location and conduct the clearance. The event in practice can take some time involving many visits to the location to fully clear it.

Exorcism

What if it is a person who is haunted or as it is termed "possessed"? It is most likely to be by a demon and not a spirit, even though spirits can momentarily take over our body. This leads to a very spiritual battle between the demon inside the person and the person cleansing the soul of the possessed. Priests and leaders of religious faiths usually carry out exorcisms. Exorcism is the practice of evicting demons or other evil spiritual entities which are supposed to have possessed (taken control of) a person. The practice is quite ancient and still part of the belief system of many religions. The person performing the exorcism, known as an exorcist, is often a priest, or an individual thought to be graced with special powers or skills. The exorcist may use religious material, such as prayers and set formulae, gestures, symbols, icons and amulets. The exorcist often invokes some benign supernatural power to actually perform the task. In general, posessed persons are not regarded as evil nor are they wholly responsible for their actions. Therefore, exorcism is generally thought of more as a cure than as a punishment. However, the two concepts are often confused in practice, and exorcism has often been used as an excuse for harsh physical punishment, or even sadism. The concept of possession by evil spirits and the practice of exorcism are ancient and widespread and thought to have their origins in prehistoric Shamanistic beliefs. The temple of Christianity includes exorcism among the miracles performed by Jesus. Because of this precedent, possession was part of the belief system of early Christianity and exorcism is still a recognized practice of Catholicism, Eastern Orthodox and some Protestant sects. In recent times, the practice of exorcism has diminished in its importance and its use decreased. This is due mainly to a greater understanding of psychology and the function and structure of the human mind. Many of the cases that in the past might have been candidates for exorcism are now accepted as suffering from a mental illness. More generally, the change in world view since the Age of Enlightenment put increased value on rationalism, materialism and naturalism and has led to a decrease in the belief of the supernatural.

Exorcism within Roman Catholicism

Solemn exorcisms, according to the Canon law of the church, can only be carried out by an ordained priest (or higher prelate) with the express permission of the local bishop, and only after a careful medical examination to exclude the possibility of mental illness. The Catholic Encyclopedia (1908) enjoined: "Superstition should not be confounded with religion, however much of their history may be interwoven, nor magic, however white it may be, with a legitimate religious rite." Signs considered indicative of demonic possession may include: speaking foreign or ancient languages of which the possessed has no prior knowledge; supernatural abilities and strength; blasphemy; and great aversion to God, the Blessed Virgin Mary, the saints and sacred objects.

The Catholic Church revised and renewed the Rite of Exorcism in January 2000. The act of exorcism is considered to be an incredibly dangerous spiritual task; the ritual assumes that possessed persons retain their free will, though the demon may hold control over their body, and involves prayers, blessings, and invocations with the use of the Document of Exorcisms and certain Supplications. (*Depart, then, transgressor. Depart, seducer, full of lies and cunning, foe of virtue, persecutor of the innocent. Give place, abominable creature, give way, you monster, give way to Christ, in whom you found none of your works. For he has already stripped you of your powers and laid waste your kingdom, bound you prisoner and plundered your weapons. He has cast you forth into the outer darkness, where everlasting ruin awaits you and your abettors.*) After the release of the horror movie *The Exorcist* in 1973 the Catholic diocese of Chicago was inundated with so many requests for exorcism that it had to add exorcists to its existing staff. The importance of the rite was reaffirmed by Pope John Paul II (who is reputed to have performed three exorcisms during his pontificate). As a result, a number of dioceses have an officially designated exorcist priest. In September 2005, Pope Benedict XVI spoke at the convention of Italian exorcists and encouraged them to "carry on their important work." Some Protestant denominations also recognize possession and exorcism, although the practice is generally less formalized than in the Catholic Church. While some denominations perform exorcism very sparingly and cautiously, some may perform it almost routinely, as part of regular religious services (especially Pentecostal denominations). Some denominations hold that all Christians have the authority to perform exorcism, not just the clergy. Exorcism is not to be taken lightly, for the battle between good and evil can physically drain the possessed victim as the demon fights to keep control of its victim.

Haunted Ireland

Halloween is a very popular time of year for people to believe in ghosts and to go out in search of them. Halloween dates back to the time of the Druids and many customs and traditions have evolved in celebration of Samhain, the festival of the dead or summer's end. In old Celtic lore, the year is divided into two halves – the dark and the light. The dark half begins at sunset on 1st November with Samhain and the light half begins at sunset on 1st May, which is the festival of Bealtaine. In past times extensive preparations were made for the sharing of a communal feast that included the dead as guests of honour. To enable the dead to come and go freely, all doors and windows were left unlatched in houses and a special cake was made exclusively for their consumption. This had to be left untouched by any mortal hand for the duration of the ritual period. Eating the food of the dead was considered sacrilege and it condemned the perpetrator to become a hungry spirit after death. It would be forever prohibited from sharing in the Samhain feast. Apart from the great feast, the dead would also have to be entertained. While the young children played games associated with the rituals of Samhain, the elders of the villages talked about the events of the past year for those who had passed on. This was believed to encourage the dead to continue to take an interest in the affairs of the living. Bonfires play a huge role in Halloween. Ancient folklore tells us that the Gods draw near to earth at Samhain. In ancient Ireland, people extinguished their hearth fires and then gathered at the ritual centre of their tribe to honour the gods with gifts and sacrifices. There the people of the village waited for the Druids to light the new fire of the year. Personal prayers in the form of objects symbolizing the wishes were cast into the blaze. At the end of the ceremony each member of the village took back to his or her home hearth a brand ignited from the new fire. Samhain fires have continued to light up the countryside down the centuries. Today we call it bonfire night. When Christianity came to Ireland, the church took a dim view of Druidic festivals and created the vigil of All Soul's Evening, or All Hallow's Eve on 31st October, the Feast of All Saints on 1st November, and All Souls Day on 2nd November.

All three days were regarded as one of the most important times of the year and were celebrated throughout Ireland with feasting, merrymaking and divination games on Halloween. Farming activities were completed by Samhain and rituals were held out of respect and remembrance for the departed on All Souls Day. The ancients believed that on this night the division between the two worlds was at its narrowest. At this time of year it is believed that hobgoblins, evil spirits and fairies cross over in great numbers. For protection against fairy mischief, holy water was sprinkled on animals. Food offerings were left outside the house. A mixture of oatmeal and salt was put on the heads of children. Iron or a dead ember from the fire was put in an infant's cot or bed, and young children were taught not to eat wild fruits on this night, for afterwards it was believed that the Puca an ancient and particularly nasty spirit went about spitting on them, while the adults were completing the chores of paying up any debts they owed. The children visited relatives and friends and were given gifts of apples and nuts. The children played games later on in the evening with the fruit. One very popular game was for all the unmarried young people to fasten an apple apiece on a string and twirl it around before a hot fire. The one whose apple fell off first would be the first to marry. The signs were not so good for the unlucky person whose apple did not fall off or was last to fall as they were destined to die unwed. In a further attempt to seal your fate an apple was peeled in one long strip and the peel thrown over the left shoulder. The shape it made as it lay on the ground showed the initial of the future spouse.

Other games included the still popular bobbing for apples in a basin of water and snap apple, a game whereby the contestants tried to take a bite out of an apple hanging on a string. Food played an important part in the celebration of Samhain. Barnbrack, a rich fruit bread was baked and various objects were wrapped and hidden in the cake. Finding a wedding ring within a slice of barnbrack meant marriage within the year and a coin signified riches. While many of the old traditions have died out, two that survive, especially in

Dublin, include the lighting of bonfires and the custom of children dressing up in costume going from house to house shouting in unison: 'Help the Halloween Party!' The tradition of carving pumpkins dates back to 18th century Ireland, when a blacksmith named Jack was denied entry into heaven. He was so evil that the devil didn't want Jack in Hell either. So Jack's spirit was condemned to wander the earthly plains for an eternity. Jack asked the Devil to give him something to light his way and was given a burning coal ember from the fires of Hell. Jack placed the ember inside a carved out turnip, hence the tradition of the carved pumpkin.

Some Famous Irish Ghosts

The Coachman

Dundermot Mound in Ballymena, Co. Antrim is said to be the home of the phantom coachman. The legend states that the phantom coach rides around the area with its ghostly driver driving on the wild horses. If you are unfortunate enough to see him and the ghostly driver asks you 'Is the bridge at Glarryford still up?' do not answer. Legend has it that if you answer the driver you will die within a year of this.

Dundermot Mound holds another sinister secret. It is reported that a gateway to Hell known as Hells Gate opens once a year releasing demons from its depths who take any witnesses straight to hell.

An Old Man Walks

Emyvale Street in Co. Monaghan is famous for its

haunting by an old man who walks the street calling out the name "Mary". Local folklore tells of the story of a woman, named Mary, robbed of her money and murdered in the same street in the 18th century. It is believed that the old man is the spirit of her husband who still walks the streets looking for his beloved wife Mary.

Spirit Girl

On Lovers Leap Rock in Dargle Valley in Bray, Co. Wicklow lives the ghost of a young girl who appears once a year on 20th June or the eve of Mid Summers Day. The story behind the haunting is that the young girl was unfaithful to her boyfriend. He is reported to have died of grief. Repenting her wrongdoing, she sat at his graveside for several days after his death till she eventually stood on the rock at lovers leap and dived into the river below, thus ending her grief and forever naming the rock Lovers Leap. Her spirit is reportedly seen once a year on the anniversary re-enacting the tragic event.

Regiment Soldier

Percy Place in Dublin is the site of the haunting of one of Sherwood Forest's regimental soldiers. The story goes that during the battle for Mount Street Bridge in the early 19th century heavy losses were sustained by the regiment and one of its guardsmen is still reported to be standing on guard.

The Hound of Glasnevin Cemetery

The ghost of a black Newfoundland dog has been seen many times at the base of a memorial statue in Glasnevin Cemetery. This statue is a memorial to Captain McNeill Boyd lost in February 1861 whilst attempting to rescue drowning seamen at Dun Laoghaire. The apparition is said to be that of Captain Boyd's devoted dog which has also been seen many times lying on his master's grave at nearby Glasnevin Cemetery. On that faithful night the Irish Sea was raging with one of the worst gales of the century. The harbour of Dun Laoghaire was littered with the debris from battered vessels. The bodies of the drowned were found scattered on the shoreline. Among those to help with the recovery of bodies was Captain Boyd in command of the coastguard vessel Ajax. That night three stricken vessels – the Neptune, the Industry and the Mary were battling huge swells as they tried to get to the shelter of the harbour. The Neptune and the Industry were smashed against the rocks whilst the Mary was shipwrecked further along the coast at Sandymount. Captain Boyd and some of his men were on the rocks rescuing men from the stricken vessels. Together with three of his men he was swept into the sea by a giant wave. When a lifeboat from the Ajax went to search for Captain Boyd and the other men, his ever-faithful Newfoundland dog was in the rescue boat also. The Irish Sea finally surrendered the body of Captain Boyd, who was brought ashore and given one of the biggest funerals ever seen in Dublin. During the funeral his faithful dog never left his master's side and walked beside the coffin. Captain Boyd's dog refused to leave his grave eventually dying of hunger. Many witnesses have reported seeing the ghost of a dog lying on the grave of Captain Boyd.

The Ghost of the Young Child

The ghostly apparition of a young child is often seen on the road outside Clongowes Wood College, in Co. Kildare. The child has over the years caused motorists to brake hard and skid. The apparition of the young child runs out onto the road in front of unsuspecting motorists who brake to avoid hitting her, but to their amazement she just vanishes. One motorist even reported the sensation of the child passing through his car.

Railway Ghost

The ghost of a railway guard inhabits the railway station at Straffan, Co Kildare. On many occasions he has been seen walking along a stretch of the local railway line at night carrying a lamp. The apparition is thought to be that of a guard on the express train that broke down on 5th October 1853 with terrible results. A luggage train following some distance behind ploughed into the express train killing sixteen people and injuring another thirty. In the following inquiry it was revealed that the warning lamp at the rear of the stopped train had gone out and the guard on duty had failed to notice this. The luggage train was unaware of the train in the station. It was too late to stop when he eventually did see it.

It is thought that the railway station ghost is that of the guard responsible for the warning light on that fateful night, and now he patrols the line at night with his lamp in atonement for his negligence to ensure that no similar accident will ever happen again.

The Lock Keeper Ghost

Portobello Harbour at Rathmines Bridge in Dublin is home to the ghost of a lock keeper who drowned himself after he was sacked for being drunk. A soldier stationed at nearby Portobello Barracks was walking from camp to meet his girlfriend one November evening when he was blinded by a brilliant light that rose from the water. The young soldier panicked, missed his footing and fell into the water, where he drowned. Two people passing by swore that the light rose from the water and took a human shape. Three years after this the same ghostly sighting was blamed for a tragedy that occurred at Portobello Harbour at 9pm of Saturday 6th April 1861. A horse-drawn bus had just dropped a passenger on the canal approach when one of the horses started to rear up. A brilliant light was seen to rise from the canal water in the form of a human. Both horses panicked with fear and backed the bus through the wooden rails of the bridge. The bus along with its horses and six passengers plunged into the cold waters and were drowned. The conductor of the bus was able to jump clear and a passing policeman pulled the driver from the water.

Antrim Castle

Although it is not standing today some remains of the castle can still be seen. It was burnt down during a fire on 28th October 1922 whilst hosting a grand ball. The castle was built in the 17th century by Dr. Colville, a royalist, for his own use. He was a puritan with a taste for the good life. His footsteps beat out a steady tattoo through the night as he does his rounds of the castle. Other nights a ghostly light flickers around the park as he searches for treasure lost for over 300 years.

Donamon Castle

Donamon Castle is reported to be one of the oldest inhabited buildings in Ireland. Recorded in the Annals of the Four Masters for the year 1154, the castle was the seat of the O'Finaghty's, the Chiefs of Clan Conway. The Clan held much of the land for miles around. Over the next 500 years the castle was attacked, destroyed, occupied and repossessed many times. In 1668 Thomas Caulfield, brother of Lord Charlemont, received the lease of the lands for 500 years. Subsequent Caulfields were prominent in local politics and many of them rose to the highest position in the Irish Bar. The last Caulfield left Donamon in 1920 and died in London in 1933. After a brief occupation by the Republican forces in 1921 it remained vacant for the next nineteen years. Donamon Castle was shunned by the local people who believed it was haunted by the ghost of a former bailiff. In 1939 the Divine Word Missionaries bought the property. The grounds were a wilderness and the castle was in a ruinous condition. Great hardship was suffered by the first community and matters were made worse by the fact that it was cut off by the war from its sister-houses on the Continent. The castle is now home to a small number of Divine Word Missionary priests.

Haunted

CONNAUGHT

King House

King House is a magnificently restored Georgian mansion
built around 1730 by Sir Henry King, whose family were
one of the most powerful and wealthy in Ireland. The
original Sir John King, a Staffordshire man, had been
granted his land for "reducing the Irish to obedience",
achieved in part through violent subjugation and by the
enforcement of the notorious anti-Catholic Penal Laws.
For the King family, establishing themselves in Ireland was
a process of determined and successful social climbing,
inheriting a baronetcy in 1755. By 1768 Edward King had
ensured his elevation to Earl of Kingston.

The grand scale of the reception gallery, its original
stone floor, tripartite windows and high vaulted ceilings
portray the impression that the house was built as a
symbol of the status and power of the King family. The
house is situated overlooking the river in Boyle town
centre, with its entrance on Main Street. King House is

built on former MacDermot Clan lands and boasts unique architectural qualities making it a building of international significance.

The Kings have been landlords for hundreds of years and perhaps the most famous, at least in this part of the country, Viscount Lorton was in charge of the estate for many decades, including the Famine years. There is evidence to say that Viscount Lorton was a fair landlord. He certainly spent a great deal of money on the estate and took care of his workers when they were ill. His wife also took an interest in the local schools and promoted the education of young children. Following a fire in 1788 the

King House

King family vacated the house. It was then leased to the British Army who bought it for £3,000 in 1795.

In his Statistical Survey of the County of Roscommon, undertaken in 1832, Isaac Weld had nothing but praise for Viscount Lorton's contribution to the environment, to his workers and to the general wellbeing of the area. The house became a military barracks and home. It became the headquarters of the Roscommon Militia of the Connaught Rangers from 1788 until 1922. It was also home to the Black and Tans who were instrumental in keeping peace after the 1916 rising until 1922. Subsequently, King House was used as a military barracks by the Irish Free State Army, who moved in after the Anglo-Irish treaty where all British troops vacated their barracks and handed them over to the newly formed Irish Army in 1922. In 1960 the main house with the north and east ground moved into private ownership. The army continued to occupy the west range and south yard. In the 1970s tenders were invited for its demolition. In 1987 it was acquired by Roscommon County Council in a very bad state of repair. Restoration work began in 1989. Artisans and craftsmen used traditional techniques and materials to restore King House to its former glory. Of particular interest is the Long Gallery with its original marble fireplace, the tripartite Venetian Windows and Vaulted Ceilings, and the Main Salon once again in use for recitals and banquets. King House is supposedly haunted by the Green Lady so much so that, a Green Lady model is part of the exhibitions in the house.

She is reported to wander her former home making sure her high standards are still being kept today as they were when she lived there.

Today King House is a museum that brings you on a journey through the life of a stately home and military barracks in Ireland.

King House Interpretive Galleries & Museum,
Main Street,
Boyle,
Co. Roscommon,
Ireland

Phone: 071 966 3242

Moore Hall

Moore Hall was built by George Moore of Ashbrook. George had amassed a considerable fortune in Alicante in Spain.

He was a wine merchant and manufactured iodine out of seaweed shipped from Galway. Moore sold his property in Alicante for £250,000 in 1784, a staggering amount of money for that time. George returned to Ireland in 1790 and set about the task of building a house. He considered several sites for the building of his house but finally settled for Muckloon Hill and ignored local advice in his choice of site. The folklore in the area was that the site was unlucky because of events that took place around 365AD to 400AD, when Brian Orbsen was King of Connaught. Towards the end of the century Brian Orbsen was killed by enemies and his Druid Drithliu escaped into hiding on Muckloon Hill. Drithliu was eventually hunted down and killed on the shores of Lough Carra. Unlucky or not for

George Moore, the house building commenced on Muckloon Hill in 1792 and was completed in 1796. Aenach Drithlind, the Royal Fort of Carra bore the Druid's name. Muckloon for the future would bear the name Moore Hall. George took the oath of allegiance to King George III. This entitled him to lease land. His estate amounted to 12,330 acres. He spent £2,200 defending his son John after the 1798 rising. George went blind from a stroke before his death. He died in November 1799, one month before his son John and is buried in Ashbrook (near Straide, Co. Mayo).

Ghosts aside, the building itself was the childhood home of the novelist also named George Moore, and a man nobody seems to have liked very much! W.B. Yeats described Moore's face as looking like it had been carved out of a turnip. Henry Arthur Jones said that he resembled "a boiled ghost." To Oliver St. John Gogarty he was simply "that egregious ass", whilst James Stephens labelled him, "the famous novelist that everybody talks about and nobody reads". But what nobody could deny for all his faults was that George Moore was indeed a talented writer, and a pillar of the local community and poor who lived on his estate. George is still fondly spoken of in the area. During the black famine in 1846, he ran a horse called Coranna in the Chester Gold Cup in England. Coranna won the cup and George used much of his winnings to alleviate the suffering of the poor in the area. It is said that no one died on the Moore estate during the famine and no evictions were ever recorded. In 1847, following his help to the poor of the area, he was elected M.P. for Mayo, heading the poll.

At the funeral of George Moore, his coffin was carried

by sixteen tenants and was attended by a large number of the poor of Mayo (with few gentry attending) – a fitting tribute.

The following is an excerpt from a letter to his mother in Chester, 6th May 1846.

My dearest Mother,

Coranna won the Chester Cup this day. We won the whole £17,000. This is in fact a little fortune. It will give me the means of being very useful to the poor this season. No tenant of mine shall want for plenty of everything this year, and though I shall expect work in return for hire, I shall take care that whatever work is done shall be for the exclusive benefit of the people themselves. I also wish to give a couple of hundred in mere charity to the poorest people about me or being on my estate, so as to make them more comfortable than they are; for instance, a cow to those who want one most, or something else to those who may have a cow, but want some other article of necessary comfort; indeed I will give £500 in this way. I am sure it will be well expended, and the horses will gallop all the faster with the blessing of the poor . . .

Lough Carra is one of Ireland's loveliest and least visited lakes and on a hill above it among the dark and gloomy woodland stand the ruins of Moore Hall. It is now an empty shell of broken walls, hollow rooms filled with toppled brick and fallen masonry, whilst its basement is a sinister labyrinth of arched corridors and dark rooms.

Locals have reported that the laughter of a young child can be heard coming from its upper floors even though most of the upper floors have now collapsed to the ground after Moore Hall was badly damaged by fire in 1923. Others have reported the feeling of being watched by someone or something from within its hollow walls, they always say there is a foreboding feeling about the house. I must admit that Moore Hall is an imposing building even though it is a sad reflection of its former glory and yes there is a constant eerie feeling about it. So strong is it that you can feel it just standing at its now locked gates as you gaze at its black hollow windows. But to date no attempt has been made to find out who or what is haunting Moore Hall.

Moore Hall is located along the banks of the eastern shore of Lough Carra, about 10 miles south-east of Castlebar.

Moore Hall,
Cong,
Co. Mayo

Renvyle House Hotel

Renvyle House is situated on Ireland's west coast, nestled between the Twelve Bens and the Atlantic Ocean. Renvyle has had a turbulent past over several centuries. It has been built, pulled down, rebuilt, burnt to ashes and rebuilt once again. Its turbulent history has only mirrored the unpredictable changes of the troubled history of Ireland. There has been a dwelling on this site since the 17th century. The O'Flaherty family occupied Renvyle Castle (now a ruin which lies only a short distance away) since the 14th century. In the 16th century it was the home of Donal O'Flaherty, husband of Grace O'Malley (Grainuaile), the Elizabethan pirate queen who is said to have lived there for a while. The story is that while she was away at sea her husband was unfaithful to her and on hearing this she launched an assault on the castle. It was not finally destroyed until the mid 17th century on the order of Cromwell by Major Myles Symes.

It is suggested that Edmund O'Flaherty built a house on the present site of Renvyle House, whose father leased the estate from the new owner Henry Blake who had bought it around 1677. It was Blake who enlarged it into a "Gentleman's Residence" replacing the thatch with slates and adding another storey to it. The walls were six feet thick, and the windows were made of thick homemade glass to withstand the Atlantic gales. Inside, the walls were panelled with oak.

On completion the wealthy rural landowner Henry Blake took up residence at Renvyle with his family. Henry Blake died in 1856. His son Edgar died in 1872 leaving the house to his widow Caroline Johanna. Caroline ran into trouble with the land league and was forced to take in paying guests. In September 1883 Renvyle House Hotel first opened its doors to the public and ceased to be a private home. The outbreak of the first world war saw another turning point for Renvyle House. With growing social unrest tourism in Ireland declined forcing the Blake's to sell Renvyle House. It was bought by Dublin poet and surgeon Oliver St. John Gogarty who used it as his holiday home. He played host to an impressive gathering of literary and artistic celebrities. At this time Irish literature was going through a particularly creative spell. Some of his guests included Augustus John, W.B. Yeats, Lady Gregory and W. Churchill. The foundation of the Irish Free State led to the Civil War, which brought disaster to Renvyle House. Gogarty was appointed as a Senator, which made him vulnerable to attacks from the Anti-Treaty Republican side, and after a failed attempt on his life, while he was in Dublin they burned Renvyle House to the ground. The Government compensated Gogarty and he rebuilt Renvyle House. Gogarty decided at this point, he could not afford to keep a large country residence and so rebuilt the house as a hotel. Renvyle House Hotel was reopened in 1930 and through the decades countless visitors came to stay.

Gogarty left Ireland to live in the United States where he wrote and lectured and returned to Renvyle on occasion. By the early 1950's it was becoming evident that the family could no longer afford to keep it and in 1953 John Allen, Donny Coyle and Michael O'Malley bought it. It remains in the Coyle family to this day. Not only does Renvyle House have a colourful history but it had a fascinating paranormal history. Renvyle was built in a H-shape with galleries connecting the two sides. One night a malevolent force moved a heavy linen chest across the door, barring outside access. Only when a workman had sawn through the bars could the family enter the room again. No maidservant ever liked to enter this part of the house alone after this incident.

One night Gogarty was sleeping in the west wing when he was woken by ponderous, limping footsteps approaching along the corridor (as if someone had one leg shorter that the other). Lighting a candle, he went to investigate this strange sound, but the moment he left his room the flame was extinguished and he found himself alone in the dark. He could not call out for help as everyone else was out of earshot. Suddenly his limbs became very heavy, "I could not strike out; it was as if I were exercising with rubber ropes," as he later put it. Fortunately, nothing further happened that night.

When one of St. John Gogarty's closest friends the poet W. B. Yeats paid a visit the paranormal activity increased dramatically. It is widely believed that Yeats and his wife were psychics and had already made contact with the spirit of a young boy in their own home of Toore, Ballylee. One night, as he sat with his companions in the oak-panelled library, the door suddenly creaked wide open. The other occupants were terrified, but Yeats raised his hand and shouted, "Leave it alone, it will go away, as it came", whereupon the invisible revenant obligingly slammed the door shut. Evan Morgan (later Lord Tredgar) was less in command of the spirits. He had recently embraced Roman Catholicism, and on being told that a particular room was haunted entered the room in an attempt to perform an exorcism. No sooner had he lit three candles and began reciting some prayers in Latin when a thick black mist filled the room, and the unfortunate Morgan was thrown to the ground. Having been dragged to safety by his friend Seymour Leslie, white faced and suffering from shock, he was treated by Dr. Gogarty. When Morgan was finally able to speak he revealed that he had seen the ghost of a pale-faced boy with large luminous eyes, dressed in brown, who was clasping his hands to his throat as if strangling himself. Morgan concluded that the boy had committed suicide in that room.

W. B. Yeats, meanwhile, held a séance in an attempt to contact the ghost. Using a method of communication called automatic writing the spirit indicated that it objected to the presence of strangers in the house. It informed Yeats that it would appear to his wife and reveal its identity. Georgia Yeats was a well-known and talented medium and felt no compunction about entering the haunted room alone. As she stood by the fireside a "vapour" mist appeared, which gradually assumed the form of a red-haired, pale-faced boy, aged around 14. "He had the solemn pallor of a tragedy beyond the endurance of a child," Mrs Yeats later told her husband. She learnt that the ghostly boy was a member of the Blake family, the original owners of the house. Now the family records of the Blake's do show that the Blakes did have a son Ethelred Henry Blake who lived from 1824-1838, this would make him 14 when he died in the house.

In the past guests have reported a sense of "someone" in their room, and several ladies have had disturbing encounters with a man, whose reflection they have seen looking over their shoulders through the mirror on the dressing table. Today Renvyle House is the perfect retreat to escape the hustle and bustle of city life.

Renvyle House Hotel,
Renvyle,
Connemara,
Co. Galway,
Ireland

Phone 095 43511
info@renvyle.com
www.renvyle.com

Rockfleet Castle

Rockfleet Castle was built around 1470 during the reign of King Henry VI though it is not in fact a castle but more a tower house. Every liege-man had to build a castle approximately 20 feet long by 16 feet wide and 40 feet high, and in doing so qualified for a subsidy from the King of £10.

The castle was probably built by the O'Malley clan. Tower houses were copied from the Norman castles and you can find many examples of this structure in the west of Ireland. A majority of these were owned by Gaelic chieftains. As with all tower houses the windows on the bottom storey are very narrow and of much less than half a metre, as this was the easiest storey to attack. However, they allow space on the inside to stand and defend. There are four windows on each wall so that they would have a view from all sides of any possible attack. On the south wall there is what is called a Slop Hole, a cavity in the wall which drained the sewage out to the exterior. Today the inside of the castle is in need of serious restoration. But if it was not for one of the castle's most famous owners it would probably have fallen into the realms of forgotten castles in Ireland.

Grace O'Malley, or as she is more commonly known as The Pirate Queen was one of the most famous of the female pirates and her history is well documented in Irish history. As a young child Grace yearned to join her father on the open sea but her mother refused saying the life of a sailor was not for young ladies. It is believed her father gave in and allowed her to travel with him to Spain.

In 1546 Grace married Donal O'Flaherty, next in line as head of the clan and possessor of the castles of Bunowen and Ballinahinch. Grace's new husband had a wicked disposition. It was thought he had murdered his sister's stepson, Walter Fada Burke, because he was a threat to the MacWilliamship. Grace had three children during their marriage, Owen, Margaret, and Murrough. Even though she had become a mother she continued her escapades and soon became better known than her husband in tribal disputes, politics, and pirating. Donal's temperament was however more suited to settling personal vendettas than ensuring the wellbeing of his clan and as a consequence his people were soon enduring genuine severe hardship. Grace stepped in to lead the O'Flaherties and by sheer force of personality made herself their chief, winning their loyalty and taking over her husband's authority as head of the clan. Soon afterwards Donal was killed by his enemies the Joyces, as they attempted to win back the island fortress that Donal had taken from them on Lough Corrib. Grace took up the battle and defeated her husband's killers. The castle became one of her favourites and she defended it against all comers including the English. The English were forced to retreat to the mainland, but Grace wasn't done with them yet. She had a trick up her sleeve. She sent one of her messengers through a secret passage from the castle to the mainland where he lit a beacon alerting her fleet. The ships put to sea, defeated the English and raised the siege.

Although by law she was entitled to a third of her late husband's estate, Grace's two sons denied her the property so Grace returned to O'Malley's land with 200 followers and set up operations on Clare Island in Clew Bay. From there she could monitor all sea traffic in and out with both protection and piracy and she made herself and her followers wealthy.

It would not be long before almost all of Clew Bay was in Grace's hands. However the one piece of property that she still desperately wanted, Rockfleet Castle, belonged to Iron Dick Burke. Grace made the necessary arrangements to marry him and in 1566 she did so with a pre-nuptial agreement that after one year if either party was unhappy they could terminate the marriage. When this time approached Grace locked herself in Rockfleet Castle and dismissed her husband, thus acquiring the castle as her own. Even though this marriage was short they still managed to have a son, Tibbot-na-Long or Theobald of the Ships. Legend has it that Grace gave birth to Theobald during a trading mission. Grace lived out her last years at Rockfleet Castle and was buried in the Cistercian Abbey on Clare Island where her remains may or may not rest today. Does the spirit of the Pirate Queen still haunt Rockfleet Castle?

Rockfleet Castle, Office of Public Works,
51 St. Stephen's Green,
Dublin 2,
Ireland

Phone: 01 6476000

Thoor Ballylee

Thoor Ballylee was built between 1275 and 1335 by the Norman De Burgo family. It is one of thirty-two such fortified residencies that span across the west of Ireland. The towers and their lands remained the property of the Catholic Burgos, or the burkes as they locally became known until the introduction of the Penal laws of the 17th and 18th centuries. This saw them and their lands being forcibly passed to the Protestant landowners. By the mid-19th century it was known as Islandmore Castle and was the family home of the Spellman family. But its most famous owner was W.B. Yeats. Yeats discovered the tower in 1896 and after the sad death of Mrs Spellman in 1902 set about buying the property for the princely sum of £35. But it was long before this that Yeats fell in love with the tower thanks to its magical association with medieval warriors of Ireland and the story of Biddy Early, who said that "there was a cure for evil between the two millwheels of

Thoor Ballylee

Ballylee". Work on restoring the tower started straight away with designs for its conversion drawn up by William Scott, professor of architecture at the National University of Ireland. Work was carried out by local joiners Patrick Connolly and Thomas Rafferty. This work was overseen by Yeats until in 1917 he went to France and it was that summer he proposed to Iseult Gonne. He was refused and went to London and Proposed to Georgina Hyde-Lees in

September of that year. Within a month the couple were married. Restoration on the tower was slow but in the summer of 1919 Yeats moved in with his wife and baby daughter Anne. The couple had a son Michael born in 1921 and 1922 William Butler Yeats named his castle by writing a letter to Olivia Shakespeare, 'what do you think of my address Thoor Ballylee? Thoor is Irish for tower and it will keep people from suspecting us of modern Gothic. I think the harsh sound of "thoor" amends the softness of the rest'. Yeats remained there until August 1928.

On 3rd August 1989 a British tourist arrived at Thoor Ballylee at approximately 5.45pm. The curator told him that the tower would be closing soon and he would only have a short while to see it. He was at the top of the tower when the caretaker came and told him that the tower was closing. The tourist asked the caretaker if he could take a picture of the window in the sitting room. The caretaker did not mind the request and re-opened the shutters for the tourist to take his picture. A keen photographer, he used a standard practical camera and 300asa speed film. No flash was used, but when he got his film developed there was a shadow of a boy standing just in front of the window in the sitting room where the caretaker had just opened it for him. Knowing that there was nobody else in the room with him that might cast a shadow into the picture, he brought it back to where he got his film developed and inquired if there was a problem with the print, that something must have been on the negative when it was being developed.

The company took back his film and had it analysed. The result was that the shadow was there in the room when the picture was taken and there is nothing wrong with either his print or negative. One theory as to who the young boy could be (and it is just a theory) arises from Yeats' visit to Renvyle House, home to fellow writer Oliver St. John Gogarty, in the early 1920s. Gogarty's house was a haunt for a literary clique and their lust and curiosity of the occult. Yeats and his wife often stayed there dabbling in séances and contacting the spirit world. Yeats quickly realised that his wife Georgina was gifted in the skill of mediumship and assisted him in his contacts into the spirit world. It was while at Renvyle house that Yates made contact with the spirit of a young boy aged fourteen. "My wife saw a pale faced, red haired boy standing before her. The apparition told her that he was Harold Blake who had killed himself in a house that previously stood where Renvyle now stood." Yeats struck up a relationship with the boy and asked him not to frighten either the owners of the property or Yeats' children. Could the spirit of this boy have followed Yeats back to Thoor Ballylee, and could it show itself to unsuspecting visitors?

Mary Callanan,
Thoor Ballylee, Gort,
Co. Galway, Ireland

Phone: 091 631436 June-September
        091 357700 October-May

LEINSTER

Áras An Uachtaráin

Located in Europe's largest and finest park comprising some 1,752 acres is Áras an Uachtaráin. The original house was designed by park ranger and amateur architect the Right Honourable Nathaniel Clements in 1751. It was bought by the British administration for the British Lord Lieutenant of Ireland to become his summer residence in the 1780s. His official residence then was in the Viceregal Apartments in Dublin Castle. It was then known as the *Viceregal Lodge,* the "out of season" residence of the Lord Lieutenant or as he was commonly known "the Viceroy". The Viceroy lived here for most of the year. During the Social Season (January to St. Patrick's Day in March) he lived in state in Dublin Castle. During its time in the Phoenix Park the Viceregal lodge was witness to some of Dublin's most famous murders. On 6th May 1882 the senior Irish civil servant, the Permanent Under Secretary Thomas Henry Burke, the newly appointed

Chief Secretary for Ireland, and Lord Frederick Cavendish were brutally stabbed to death using surgical knives, as they walked though the Phoenix Park in Dublin en route to the Viceregal Lodge. Their attackers used very short knives and they were brutally hacked to death. The then Lord Lieutenant and the Earl Spencer described hearing screams before witnessing a man running to the Lodge grounds shouting "Lord Frederick Cavendish and Mr. Burke have been killed". Responsibility for the assassinations was claimed by a small republican organisation called *The Invincibles*. In the aftermath, the Irish nationalist leader Charles Stewart Parnell offered to resign from parliament in protest at what he called "these vile murders", an offer turned down by the British Prime Minister, William Ewart Gladstone.

There have been many improvements and additions to the house over the years. The most noteworthy being the establishment of formal gardens by Decimus Burton in the 1840s, the addition of the East Wing in 1849 for the state visit of Queen Victoria and the installation of Dublin's mains gas supply in 1852 and electricity in 1908.

In 1911 the house underwent a large extension for the visit of King George V and Queen Mary who performed the opening of the Irish Parliament in Dublin.

With the creation of the Irish Free State in 1922 the office of Lord Lieutenant was abolished. The new state planned to place the new representative of the Crown, Governor-General Tim Healy in a new but smaller residence. Because of death threats he received from the anti-treaty IRA he was housed in the Viceregal Lodge for what was to be a temporary residence. It remained the residence of the Governor-General of the Irish Free State until 1932, when the new Governor-General Domhnall Ua Buachalla was installed in a specially hired private mansion to the south of Dublin. The Viceregal Lodge remained empty and unused for some years until the office of the President of Ireland was created in 1937. In 1938, the first President, Douglas Hyde lived there temporarily while plans were made to build a new presidential palace on the grounds. The outbreak of World War II saved the building, which had been renamed *Áras an Uachtaráin* (meaning *house of the president* in Irish), from demolition. The plans for its demolition and the design of a new residence were put on hold. By 1945 it had become too closely identified with the presidency of Ireland to be demolished, though its poor condition meant that extensive demolition and rebuilding of parts of the building were necessary, notably the kitchens, servants' quarters and chapel.

The first President, Douglas Hyde lived in the residential quarters on the first floor of the main building. Later Presidents moved to the new residential wing attached to the main house that had been built for the visit of King George V in 1911. Though Áras an Uachtaráin is not as palatial as many European royal and presidential palaces, with only a handful of state rooms, the state drawing room, large and small dining rooms, the President's Office and Library, a large ballroom and a presidential corridor lined with the busts of past presidents, and some fine 18th and 19th century bedrooms above, all in the main building, it is a relatively comfortable state residence.

Áras an Uachtaráin has seen some famous visitors through its life, some of whom were visiting British monarchs, notably Queen Victoria and George V, American Presidents hosted include Presidents John F. Kennedy, Richard Nixon, Ronald Reagan and Bill Clinton, all of Irish descent. Other famous visitors to Áras an Uachtaráin have been Princess Grace of Monaco and her husband Prince Rainier III. King Baudouin of the Belgians, King Juan Carlos and Queen Sophia, Pope John Paul II, Prince Charles and Prince Philip also visited.

Áras an Uachtaráin has another guest that pops in from time to time. This guest is the Ghost of Young Winston Churchill. There are stories of a small boy, allegedly a young Winston Churchill, running about the building. Churchill grew up there as a child when his grandfather, the Duke of Malborough, was Lord Lieutenant. It was supposed to be one of young Winston's favourite places. So it is not surprising that he would want to revisit his more happier memories as he returns from the spirit world.

Áras an Uachtaráin is open Saturdays only. Free admission tickets are issued at the Phoenix Park Visitor Centre on the day. Group and/or advance booking is not permitted.

Áras an Uachtaráin,
Phoenix Park,
Dublin 8

Phone: 01 617 1000

Ardgillan Castle

The original demesne consists of the ancient town lands of Kilmainham, Ardgillan and Baltray. This district was originally controlled by the Gaelic O'Casey family and later the Earl of Tyrconnell. However, the period between 1600 and 1700 saw a great change in the pattern of land ownership in Ireland due to the confiscation and redistribution of land after the Cromwellian and Williamite wars. Although we refer to Ardgillan as a castle it is a large country-style house with castellated embellishments. Originally named "Prospect", the central section of the castle was built in 1738 by Robert Taylor with the west and east wings added in the early 19th century.

Initially the site where the castle stands was heavy woodland, the name Ardgillan being derived from the Irish "Ard Choill" meaning High Wood. The land was cleared by out-of-service soldiers and itinerant workers who in return for their hard labour received one penny a

Ardgillan Castle

day wages, sleeping accommodation and one meal per day. The castle consists of two storeys over a basement. The ground and first floors were the living accommodation. The west and east wings were servants quarters and estate offices. The basement was the service area comprising of the kitchen and stores, with the family sleeping quarters on the upper floors.

The gardens are in two main parts, the formal garden to the west of the house and the walled garden to the north-west constructed by the Scottish firm Mckenzie and Moncur in the 1880s. The walled garden was a typical Victorian-style kitchen garden used to supply the castle with fruit, vegetables and cut flowers.

In 1658 Ardgillan was owned by the wine merchant Robert Usher of Crumlin, but by 1737 the property had been acquired by the Reverend Robert Taylor, one of the Headfort Taylors, whose grandfather had collaborated with Sir William Petty in the mid 17th century. Ardgillan remained the family home of the Taylors for more than 200 years until 1962 when the estate was sold to Heinrich Pott of Westphalia Germany. In 1982 Dublin County Council purchased Ardgillan Demesne and it is now owned by Fingal County Council. One surviving feature still intact in the garden is the Yew Walk which is to the south of the house. This was planted in the 1800s during the time of Marianne Taylor, wife of Rev. Henry Edward Taylor. It was a favourite walking place for Captain Edward Taylor (1863-1938).

Local folklore has it that a shadowy figure sometimes seen here is the ghost of a member of the Taylor family.

The Lady's Stairs, a set of steps leading down to the sea at Barnageeragh strand just over the pedestrian footbridge above the Balbriggan to Skerries Road, is named after reports of a ghostly figure of a "Lady" seen here from time to time on the bridge that crosses the railway line to the ladies stairs. The "Lady" is reported to be the ghost of Edith Connolly who drowned in the sea just at the ladies stairs at Barnageeragh, while she went for a swim one November morning in late 1853. An account of her death was recorded in a letter by Lady Fanny Kemble.

33 Via Delle Mercedi, Rome
Thursday, December 22, 1853.

Your kind and pleasant letter, dear Arthur, which I have just been reading over to see if it contains anything more especially to be answered, ends with a question about that poor wretched lady L–d, and a hope that she was not much related either by blood or affection to my dear Harriet St Leger. Here, close by me, lies a letter I received yesterday from her, full of the most painful details of the catastrophe, which occurred at her home, Ardgillan Castle (luckily she was absent from it at the time), where I was staying last autumn twelve months, and made acquaintance with the unfortunate young woman whose death has, of course, given an association of horror to the beautiful place, which it will be long before any of the family will be able to overcome. Maria, my friend Harriet's eldest niece, was on the cliffs, and witnessed her cousin's death without being able to render or procure assistance for her. She received the corpse in her arms, when it was at last rescued from the sea, and has ever since been suffering from a most horrible nervous affection of the eyes, which causes her to see half of everyone's face like the livid and swollen half of her drowned cousin's face, as she last saw it. Is not that a wretched penalty to pay for having been the most unwilling witness of such a tragedy?

Ardgillan Castle has a fascinating and rich ghostly history. Apart from the white Lady on the stairs and the shadowy figure at the yew walk, there are also reports of a lady dressed in white. The door at the rear of Ardgillan looks out onto a terrace lined with yew trees and is connected to the front door through a series of passageways. One of these passageways leads down to a glass door which leads to the cellars.

On one occasion the gardener's two sons were working on the terrace when they heard footsteps coming down a flight of stairs in the house. The footsteps seemed to approach the terrace door then suddenly stopped. Suspecting they had an intruder, the two men looked in through a window but saw nothing. They then checked all the doors in the castle and found them locked. Later that day they told their father their story. He was amused by it but later he told his sons a story of his own. A few years earlier, he returned to the castle late at night carrying some vegetables in a basket. He entered the house by the terrace door and walked along the passage towards the kitchen. Passing the glass cellar door, to his surprise he saw a woman dressed in white standing behind it. Thinking that she had been locked in he then made a move to open the door to let her out, but the lady just vanished. Puzzled, he continued on into the kitchen, leaving the basket behind him on the table. On his return the figure was there again standing behind the glass door. Once more the gardener tried to make contact with her, but just like before she disappeared.

A lady in white was seen walking down the main stairs of the castle across the inner hallway and out the front door. Other staff in the castle have reported seeing a shadow-like figure passing them on the staircase. Just off what is now the reception and café entrance, on one of these occasions, a staff member thought it was one of her colleagues and called out to her but she was answered from a totally different direction to which the shadow passed. I must point out that they were the only two in the castle at the time.

Ardgillan Castle is a beautifully preserved castle rich in Irish history. But as you visit the castle and walk through its many rooms and as you stroll through its gardens, keep a watchful eye out for you just might be graced with a glimpse of Captain Edward Taylor at the yew walk or you just might see a lady dressed in white pass you by.

Ardgillan Castle,
Balbrigan,
Co. Dublin

Phone: 01 8492212

Charleville Forest Castle

Charleville Forest Castle is one of the finest gothic castles in Ireland. Designed by Francis Johnston for Charles William Bury the first earl of Tullamore, the building of the castle took Lord Bury and his wife Charlotte Maria a further twelve years to complete. In fact Charles and Lady Charleville moved into the castle long before the builders moved out. During the building Lady Charleville received a letter from Lady Louisa Connolly, "I am glad to hear that you have begun your castle for I think there are few occupations more entertaining than building". The extravagant décor of the interior of this magnificent castle is only rivalled by its awe-inspiring exterior. As you drive through the winding oak forest the castle rears suddenly in front of you. A huge heavy corbelled archway marks the entrance of the castle and as you approach the entrance the huge circular tower to your left rises high above the battlements; to your right the octagonal tower stands bold and threatening. As you stand at the doorway you become aware of "loops" each side; these were for archers to shoot their arrows through at any unsuspecting intruder. As you enter you are met with the splendour of the main staircase which leads up to the main dining hall, which spans the full 120 feet of the castle length. Every room of this main level is gloriously decorated with beautifully plastered ceilings.

Young Charles Bury's birthday celebrations were even more extravagant than his castle. For his 21st birthday a hot air balloon (rather than soaring into the air) crashed and burned the town of Tullamore. It crashed into the barracks chimney and set its thatched roof on fire. This wild birthday celebration cost young Bury £550 in compensation. The Burys had two sons and three daughters, but one of his daughters Lady Harriet (at the young age of eight) tragically met her death in the castle. She was sliding down the staircase from her nursery in April 1861 when she lost her balance and fell to her death. This staircase is now known as Harriet's staircase and the present trustees and several guests have reported hearing the voice of a young girl playing on this very staircase. But this is not the only spirit that is reported to haunt Charleville Castle.

Constance Heavey Seaquist, former chatelaine and mother of the present trustee Bonnie Vance, reported seeing figures closely resembling Charles William Bury and Francis Johnston. One morning at around 3am, Constance was woken to find them leading a ghostly parade across her bedroom in the tower. The parade consisted of a woman in a black hood, a little girl and a group of around seventeen monks or druids who encircled her bed and appeared to be blessing her. But it's in the dungeon area of the castle that its menacing spirit dwells; of a man by the name of O'Reilly.

O'Reilly is reported to have been a jailer for the castle who tortured followers of Robert Emmet between 1801-1802 in the dungeon of the castle. Robert Emmet's rising collapsed as a result in 1803. I have visited the castle many times and spent a lot of time in the dungeon and surrounding area of the dungeon and have found no malevolent spirit there of any kind. But having said this, the dungeon is a scary part of the castle. My only paranormal experience in this area came one night while using my digital camcorder. I was standing just outside the entrance to the dungeon when two orbs floated past me and headed into the dungeon. This I caught on camcorder and have had analyzed. The findings were that it was not dust particles as dust can be seen moving, so therefore it must have been an orb.

Charleville Forest Castle holds a very special place in my heart as it was the first location I ever investigated. Despite the abundance of ghosts that roam its corridors one always seems to leave it with a sense of sheer wonder at its beauty. Back along the driveway one comes upon the magnificent "King Oak" the massive girth of which testifies to its venerable age. Yet its majestic splendour is tinged with a fearsome reputation, for it is maintained that, whenever one of its branches fell, a member of the Charleville family would die. In May 1963, a huge bolt of lightning smashed into it and shattered its trunk from top to bottom. Although the mighty oak survived its attack, two weeks later Colonel Charles Howard Bury (the head of the family and the last of the line to own the castle) suddenly dropped dead.

Charleville Forest Castle,
Tuallmore,
Co. Offaly

Phone: 0506 23040

Clonony Castle

Clonony was built in 1500 by the McCoughlan clan. The Mc Coughlans built many castles in this area known as "the land of fair castles". Clonony would be the finest surviving example of these castles. It was built near the Shannon Harbour, a busy port on the Shannon River. On the grounds of Clonony Castle under a spreading Hawthorne tree is the Bullen Stone. This large limestone slab was quarried for the remains of Elizabeth and Mary Bullen, nieces of the ill-fated wife of Henry VIII, Anne Boleyn, and cousins to Queen Elizabeth I. When Henry desired the marriage to Anne he elevated her father to royal status by making him Earl of Ormond and Wiltshire. With this Ormond Earldom came several Irish castles, one of which was Clonony Castle. The castle has many colourful associations and just a few yards from its main entrance lies a large limestone slab which bears an inscription telling us that it was the tombstone of Elizabeth and Mary Bullen. A massive limestone grave slab, built between 1700 and 1900, with dimensions 2.2 x 1.2 x 0.27m, is situated under a tree approximately seven metres from the south-west corner of the tower house. This impressive slab of a light blue to grey ornamental carboniferous limestone was inscribed in English. However, most of the carved inscription has disappeared due to superficial dissolution. Calcite dissolution is also evident along natural joints and stylolites. This has led to the appearance of grooves on the surface of the slab.

From other information on this slab we know these people to be relations of Anne Boleyn, one of the wives of Henry VIII and also Anne's daughter who eventually became Queen Elizabeth I. In the 1620s the castle was granted to Matthew de Renzi. His relationship with the Mc Coughlans was by no means a curious one. Initially he spoke of being ostracised by them (since they had lost their lands to him), but somehow relations improved to the extent that de Renzi decided to learn the Irish language. His tombstone in Athlone credits him with writing a dictionary in the Irish tongue.

In the 1830s, the castle belonged to Edmond Molony, a barrister-at-law. A description of Clonony in 1838 states that Molony was a counsellor who "was bred to the law and retained a very proper veneration for it". Edmond kept two flag staffs on the top of the battlements of Clonony Castle which he used for the pleasure of commemorating his professional triumphs. Edmond's wife died in January 1839 and was interred in St. George's Chapel in London. The epitaph on her monument erected by her husband is extremely long, having more than 300 words, including the immortal lines:

> She was hot, passionate and tender,
> A highly accomplished lady,
> And a superb drawer in water colours.

Today Clonony Castle tower is in an excellent state of preservation with one exception, the barrel vaulted ceiling is now at risk of collapsing. Water is penetrating the stonework, leeching precious lime mortar with it. It's a race between the lime mortar and the government agencies.

Clonony Castle is open to the public as restoration work continues. Sadly this work is dependent on the Irish weather and availability of craftsmen. There are no specific opening hours, although most of the summer is a hive of activity and the gates to the castle are open with a suggested donation toward conservation of the building. This great square ruin of a tower in the middle of Offaly certainly looks creepy enough, and the connection with Anne Boleyn and the fact that two of her cousins are buried in a cave beneath the castle would encourage that sense. The ghost that people see is that of a man standing on top of the tower in old-fashioned dress. His identity remains a mystery, but he is still regularly seen by passing motorists at night, who have described a tall, thin, almost skeletal figure, surrounded by a hazy luminous light.

Clonony Castle,
Shannon Harbour,
Birr, Co. Offaly

Collins Barracks, Dublin

In 1700 the Irish Parliament established an administrative structure to control its barracks network. In the same year Thomas Burgh was appointed surveyor general and chief engineer of the building of a barracks that would accommodate all the armed forces in Dublin.

In 1704 he purchased the site and designed the new barracks that was also to include a military hospital. The building of the barracks only took three years to complete and in April 1707 the first regiment of Col. Pierce Foot began to arrive in the Barracks. It was known then as the Royal Barracks and the largest in Europe housing 1500 men and 150 horses. In 1746 the Royal Barracks got its own chapel long after it was requested in 1711. By 1726 troops had regular stoppages made from their earnings to pay for a surgeon. This was because soldiers regularly suffered from malnutrition and scurvy, as well as the regular wounds received in war. Life in the barracks was harsh and it was a necessity to train hard fearless fighting men. The sleeping quarters for the early troops were six men to a room sleeping two to a bed. Beside and hung above their beds were their arms, boots, furniture and uniforms. The men would also cook their food in their own rooms, but because of all the deductions that included washing of sheets and the keep of their horses, the poor soldiers could only afford a fine banquet of rotten bread, poor veal, cheese and buttermilk which was half water anyway. If this wasn't bad enough the discipline routine was even harder. As soon as daylight broke the men were woken by the sound of the reveille, a military waking signal sound on a bugle and drum. An hour after this the second drum would beat and the cavalry would clean out the stables, feed and clean their horses. At 6am in summertime when the third drum sounded they would bring the horses for water.

This regimental discipline would continue all day until it was the end of another day with the sounding of the final reveille. Life was so harsh that some soldiers attempted to desert the regiment by escaping. Discipline was so harsh that one case that caused a stir and attracted attention was that of David Blakeney. Blakeney was from a nearby barracks and complained on behalf of his fellow soldiers that when he enlisted he was not assigned a complete uniform but given an old coat and ragged clothes to wear, yet he was still stopped the full cost for a full uniform.

His punishment was to be transferred to the Royal Barracks and to be given 500 lashes of the knotted whip. Following a plea for leniency to the lord lieutenant his number of lashes were reduced and on 4th January he was ordered into the square of the barracks, and there ordered to strip for flogging. Blakeney knew the suffering he was about to endure and he had other ideas in mind. He drew a knife and stabbed himself in the stomach three times. He was taken to the infirmary to recover from his wounds, after which he was given his sentence of lashes. At this point he was refused medical attention and forced to walk back to his own barracks. As with all military barracks life for officers was vastly different.

Not for them two to a bed and cramped conditions, but each officer had his own room with a fireplace and a nicely sprung bed. By the 1790s the conditions for the soldiers had improved with several extensions being added to the barracks. Life within the barracks was harsh for the soldiers, but life for its prisoners was even worse. When the 1798 rebellion erupted the soldiers of the Royal Barracks earned the reputation for merciless flogging and subsequent executions of the prisoners. It is believed that because of the number of court-martials being carried out each day that gallows were erected on Arbour Hill, just outside the walls of the barracks, and on the bridges of the River Liffey. The bodies were buried in a mass grave just outside the main gate of the barracks where a memorial plot now stands. Some famous prisoners that were executed at Arbour Hill were Matthew Tone in 1798, Bartholomew Teeling in 1798, also Wolfe Tone in 1798 who dressed in his blue French Army uniform and with a tricolour cockade in his hat as he told his court-martial that he had attempted to establish an independence for his country. Wolfe Tone was told that he was not to receive a firing squad but to be hanged like all the rest. Furious to be denied a soldier's death he was mortally wounded in the neck. In 1916 the Royal Barracks yet again answered the call to fight its own Irish on home ground. For it was the 2nd Sherwood regiment that escorted the leaders of the rising to their court-martial. But by far the biggest moment in the barracks' history was yet to come, for after the signing of the Anglo-Irish treaty in 1921 the Irish Free State was given the right to establish its own defence forces. On 1st February 1922 Michael Collins wrote to the commander in chief of British Forces saying that the provisional government would take over all the barracks occupied by the British forces. The last of these barracks to be handed over was the Royal Barracks in Dublin and on 17th December 1922 General Sir Neville Macready took the salute of his men as they marched out of the barracks and down the quays where they headed back to England. The commander-in-chief General Richard Mulcahy and the chief of staff General McMahon took the first salute of the Free State Army and signalled an end to the Royal Barracks now renamed Collins Barracks. From December 1922 till April 1997 Collins Barracks remained an Irish Army Barracks when Brig. Gen. Colm Mangan of the Eastern Command took the salute of the 5th Infantry Battalion as they marched from the barracks. Collins Barracks is the longest serving military barracks in Europe and during its time was home to Col Pierce's Foot 1707; Ferwick's Regiment, Husard's Regiment and 5th dragoons 1711; Purcell's Regiment and 3rd King's own Hussars 1721; Cameronian Regiment and 18th Hussars 1741; 37th foot Hampshires and Royal Irish Regiment 1771; 68th Regiment

1798; 71st Foot, 76th Foot, and 11th hussars 1799; Royal Irish Fusiliers and 12th Lancers 1811; 28th Regiment Foot and 66th Foot Berksires 1831; Grenadier Guards and Royal Irish Regiment 1867; 2nd Battalion Welsh Fusiliers 1882; East Lancaster Regiment 1901; 2nd Battalion Sherwood Foresters 1916; 2nd South Lancashire Regiment and 2nd Battalion Wilshire regiment 1917; 15th Infantry Battalion National Army; 6th Field Artillery Regiment 1940; 6th Field Artillery Regiment 1944; 5th Infantry Battalion.

With such a long and distinguished life it's not surprising that some of the Royal Barracks/Collins Barracks former occupants have chosen to remain behind, to remind us of its gruesome past. Like the reporting of a ghostly figure wandering its parade yards witnessed by both military personnel when it was a barracks and by museum staff today. Could this be the spirit of young Thomas Higgins who tried to escape military life in 1708 by running away from the army? When Thomas was caught he was taken to waste ground beside the barracks called Oxmantown Green to the right hand side of the barracks where he was executed by firing squad. Then there is the ghost on the third floor, the ghost of a soldier who reportedly hanged himself. I have tried to trace this piece of information but so far I have found no account of a soldier who hanged himself on the third floor. But staff have reported an uneasy feeling on the same third floor and do not like to be up there alone.

Collins Barracks,
Benburb Street, Dublin 7, Ireland

Phone: 01 6777444

Drimnagh Castle

Nestled behind the Christian Brothers school on the Longmile Road in Dublin is Drimnagh Castle. The core part of the castle was built by Norman De Barnewall and dates back to the early 13th century. The De Barnewall family were granted lands by King John and also included Terenure land and Ballyfermot land. These land grants were systematic and part of the plan to secure the Anglo-Norman hold on Ireland. By placing strong barons and knights on such lands and charging them with the responsibility of building castles on them and keeping armed men at them, De Barnewall's tenure on the land and Drimnagh Castle lasted for 400 years. The oldest part of the castle is the "rectangular keep" which dates back to the early 13th century. This would have been surrounded by a walled enclosure with towers at each corner. The adjoining battlements with lookout posts were built in the 16th century. The original drawbridge was replaced by a stone bridge in 1780 and the extension wing to the castle was built in the last century. As you enter the castle through the main doorway you cannot but notice a hole above your head. This is called a "murder hole" and through this hole boiling water and other projectiles such as arrows and stones were hurled down on unsuspecting attackers. This door would lead into an "under croft", a low dark room with arrow slits for further attack should the enemy breach the main door. A spiral stone staircase leads up to the great hall. The great hall was a two storey high room with a thick oak beamed roof.

It is the only Irish castle still to be surrounded by a flooded moat, a very picturesque feature and a great natural defence feature. It is now stocked with fish. But one of the most attractive aspects of Drimnagh today is the garden, a formal 17th century layout with box hedges, yews, mop head laurels and an alley of hornbeam.

The last family to reside at the castle was the Hatch family who ran a dairy farm from the castle. In 1954 the Hatch brothers donated the castle to the catholic church. The Christian Brothers took over and lived in the castle whilst the school and new living quarters were being built. In 1958 the brothers moved out of the castle into the newly built quarters and the castle fell into decline for the next 30 years and was in grave danger of being demolished. In 1986 a plan was put together for the conservation and restoration of the castle and a restoration committee was set up. An international training exchange programme using traditional methods of craftsmanship was used in the restoration of the castle which opened to the public five years later.

The castle is reputed to be haunted by the spirit of Eleanora De Barnewall. She was an orphaned niece who lived in the castle with Hugh De Barnewall and his son Edmond. The De Barnewall family had several arch enemies, one of whom was the O'Byrne clan from the Dublin and Wicklow mountains. The O'Byrnes made several castle raids on Drimnagh Castle. Sir Hugh De Barnewall was a powerful man for his time and was working towards peace with the Irish. He organised a feast and called a gathering of the O'Byrne and the O'Toole clans to discuss peace. It was at this feast that Sean O'Byrne saw and fell in love with Eleanora and she with him. But Eleanora was betrothed to Edmond De Barnewall. Hugh forbid them to ever see each other again and locked Eleanora in her room until her wedding day. This infuriated Sean and he conjured up his own plan to make Eleanora his. On the day of her wedding, as the wedding party made its way to St Patrick's Cathedral the O'Byrne clan attacked. Sean made for his arch rival Edmond. A furious battle ensued between them resulting in Edmond being struck down. Sir Hugh, seeing his only son being brutally struck down, charged towards Sean and vowed not to retreat until he got his revenge. Edmond was fatally wounded and was carried away from the battle. Eleanora locked herself in her room in despair at the death of her true love Sean. One morning Eleanora disappeared, a search of the castle and grounds proving futile. Her disappearance remained a misery until one day a member of the O'Byrne clan visited Sean's grave only to find the body of Eleanora stretched across his grave. They say she died of a broken heart. It is said that if you are in

129

the castle after dark you can hear Eleanora sobbing and calling out the name of her lover to come and collect her.

Eerie crying and a negative energy on the stairwell, the feeling of being watched from someone on the minstrels gallery and the strange smell of lilies in the oratory are just a few of the many reported happenings at Drimnagh castle.

Drimnagh Castle,
Long Mile Road,
Dublin 12

Phone: 01 4502503

The Drumgoff Barracks

When Michael Dwyer, leader of the 1798 Rebellion, sought refuge in the densely wooded Wicklow mountains, the British soldiers carved a road through the forest across the mountain from Rathfarnham to Aughavanagh in an attempt to capture him and his men. The chief engineer of the road was Alexander Taylor.

It was at Glenmalure that they erected Drumgoff Barracks, now the youth hostel at Aughavanagh. The Barracks were built with the intention of flushing Dwyer and his followers out of the Dublin mountains. Michael Dwyer was born in the Glen of Imaal in 1772. He joined the Society of United Irishmen and took part in the rebellion in Wexford in 1798. Following the defeat of the United armies in Wexford, Dwyer retreated into the vast wilderness area of the Wicklow Mountains. From here he carried out a spirited resistance to the Crown's authorities for over five years, as a leader of the remnants of the rebel army. Dwyer was known as the "Master of the Mountains"; this was due to his extraordinary knowledge of his native terrain.

Dwyer had arranged terms with the authorities and when he gave himself up he expected that he and his entourage would be granted safe passage to America. He was held in Kilmainham Jail until August 1805, when he was transported to Australia. After the building ceased to be used as a military barracks it became a hunting lodge for Charles Stewart Parnell, but one of its more sinister occupants was Hempenstall. Hempenstall was a large man of at least seven foot in height and was an object of hate among the locals and the rebellion troops. Hempenstall

Drumgoff Barracks

earned himself the name of the "walking hangman" for he used to lift his victims up in the air over his head by a short rope until the life was extinguished out of them. But retribution for his own death was as violent as that of his many victims. A group of surviving rebels from the 1798 Rebellion lay in ambush at the gates of the Barracks for Hempenstall, who fell to his death with no mercy from the friends of so many of his victims. The gateway still stands there today as a silent reminder to the violent past of this peaceful countryside. But it is at this very gate that countless bear witness to a tall frightening figure that is seen at the gate but then vanishes. The Drumgoff Barracks are owned by the Irish Youth Hostel Association An Oige and is located beside Glenmalure Youth Hostel.

From Laragh, follow the Wicklow Way trail to Drumgoff Bridge, turn up the Glenmalure Valley and follow the lane to the mountain hut.

Contact details for the Drumgoff Barracks are:
Glenmalure Hostel
Glenmalure,
Greenane,
Co. Wicklow.

Phone 01 8304555
Bookings: mailbox@anoige.ie

Dublin Castle

Dublin Castle stands on the high ridge at the junction of the River Liffey and its tributary, the Poddle (now underground). This would have served as a natural moat for the early castle on the site.

In the year 930, a Danish Viking fortress stood on this site and part of the old town's defences are still on view in the under croft. Their settlement then called Dyflinn, quickly became the main Viking military stronghold and centre for trading in slaves and silver in Ireland. This power was broken after the Battle of Clontarf in 1014 when they and their allies were heavily defeated by an Irish army under the command of King Brian Boru. Their reign lasted till 1169 when neither the Irish nor the Vikings could withstand the Norman invasion. The Vikings were defeated and forced out of Ireland and the Normans became the next occupiers of Dublin. They set about expanding and strengthening the walls of the town of Dublin. In 1171 Henry II King of England invaded Ireland to consolidate Strongbow's claims to the crown. Anglo-Norman rule of Ireland began.

In August 1204 King John of England commanded that there should be a larger and stronger castle on the site with strong walls and good ditches purposely for the defence of the city and for the administration of justice and safe custody of treasure. This work was completed by 1230 and the Great Courtyard (Upper Castle Yard) of today corresponds closely with the fortification. The structure of the Dublin Castle we know today began to take shape. There were also several towers constructed as part of its outer defences.

In 1565 the new Lord Deputy Henry Sidney moved his household into Dublin Castle. From then on Dublin Castle became the control centre for the vicious wars and religious persecution against the Irish Chieftains and the Old English Catholics, many of whom were of Norman stock. By the end of Queen Elizabeth's reign, the whole island of Ireland had been conquered and new English landholding, political and social structures imposed.

In the fire on 7th April 1684 much of medieval Dublin Castle, including the old Parliament House, burnt down. Connecting buildings and halls were purposely blown up by castle staff to prevent the flames reaching the gunpowder store in the Powder Tower and the State Papers in the Bermingham Tower. The castle was rebuilt by King James and Dublin Castle entered a new era in its life. Much of what we know as present-day Dublin Castle dates from this era. After the 1798 rebellion by the United

Dublin Castle

Irishmen the Irish parliament was extinguished, and its legislative powers transferred to London. Dublin Castle's role as policy maker virtually ceased and the post of Viceroy degenerated to that of figurehead.

Viceroy Wellesley moved his household to the new Viceregal Lodge in the Phoenix Park (now the Irish

137

PAUL FENNELL

President's official residence) in the 1820s. The Castle was then mainly used by government departments, the army and the police. The Easter Rebellion of 1916 marked the beginning of the end of British rule. On 6th December 1921 the Anglo Irish Treaty was signed and Ireland became the Irish Free State ending seven and a half centuries of English rule. The rebel military chief-of-staff Commander Michael Collins arrived in the Upper Yard of Dublin Castle on 16th January 1922 to receive the handover of the Castle from the last Lord Lieutenant Fitz Alan. Unlike other castles in Ireland, Dublin Castle had a comparatively uneventful history and only ever had to endure one siege. This was when Silken Thomas made an unsuccessful and rather disorganised attempt to capture it in 1534. For many centuries it was the official residence of the Lords Deputy and Lords Lieutenant of Ireland, the home of State councils, and sometimes Parliament and the Law Courts.

In the mid 19th century a member of the Lord Lieutenant of Ireland's staff reported seeing the ghosts of two file clerks walking through his office carrying papers and chatting before exiting through a door that was long sealed up. The same two 'ghostly visitors' have supposedly been witnessed by people working in the Castle. On one occasion they were heard talking about Theobald Wolfe Tone, an Irish rebel executed after a failed rebellion in 1798. This story appeared in the Garda review magazine of November 1955. Gardai stationed at Dublin Castle were persecuted by a ghost that switched on and off the lights. When he had finished his training Garda Lowe was given sleeping quarters in the castle. Some fourteen men slept in the castle at that time. He was asleep when the light in his room was switched off. Thinking the others were playing a joke on him he jumped out of bed and switched it on and looked out past the door, but nobody was there. After he returned to bed the same thing happened again. Then he heard someone shovelling coal into the kitchen range. The range had only the capacity to hold three shovels of coal but the shovelling continued on and on. Garda Lowe got out of bed and went to investigate the shovelling coming from the kitchen. When he was outside the kitchen he could still hear the shovelling, but when he slowly opened the door it stopped. There was no-one in the kitchen and the fire in the range was nearly out. No fresh coal had been put on the range for hours and the shovel was in its usual position against the wall.

Dublin Castle,
Dublin 2

Phone: 01 677 7129

Foulksrath Castle

Foulksrath Castle is a 15th century Norman tower house located in Jenkinstown in Co. Kilkenny. Built by the Purcell clan who also constructed several other tower castles nearby, this lovely 15th century Norman tower house has many medieval features, including a magnificent dining room with enormous fireplaces and a spiral staircase leading to upper floors. After over three centuries as owners, the family was reduced to living as peasants in the castle stables after the castle was confiscated by Oliver Cromwell and given to his officers after the Cromwellian conquest of Ireland.

It presently functions as a hostel in the An Óige (Irish Youth Hostel Association) network and claims to be the oldest hostel in Ireland.

The castle was scheduled to be demolished in 1946 but was saved by the local community, restored and re-opened as a hostel in 1948.

Foulksrath Castle is well preserved with most of the

Foulksrath Castle

outer wall and some ancillary structures also surviving in
addition to the main tower. A pitched roof has been added
over the centre of the tower. The tower's battlement has
been preserved and is still accessible. Inside, the dormitory
rooms house up to 52 visitors. A kitchen and bathroom
facilities as well as a medieval decorated dining hall have
also been added. The four storeys are connected by a
narrow spiral staircase.

Stories have circulated that Foulksrath Castle is
haunted by the daughter of the original owner who was
supposedly killed in the tower, and a guard who was

originally stationed there. The story tells of the daughter who fell in love with an Irish boy against her father's wishes and was locked away by her father in the "cuckoo nest" within the castle to stop her from seeing him. Eventually the father in a fit of rage murdered his daughter to prevent her seeing her beloved.

Her ghost still walks the castle halls, probably looking for her long lost lover and is accompanied by the smell of wild flowers.

The guard, on the other hand, fell asleep while on duty. He was discovered by his superiors and his punishment at that time was death, so he was thrown from the battlements. Once a year it is reported his footsteps are heard as he walks the castle still carrying out his duties to make amends for his inappropriate actions. Foulksrath Castle has become famous as Ireland's most haunted hostel and has the highest reported accounts of noise and movements. A stay in the castle is a must for any budding or serious ghost hunter.

Foulksrath Castle,
Jenkinstown,
Co Kilkenny,
Ireland

Phone: 056 7767674
Bookings: mailbox@anoige.ie

The Ghost of Jonathan Swift

In 1996 I worked with a security company and was assigned to St Patrick's Hospital in Dublin. I worked both twelve hour night and day shifts, but it was during the night shifts that St Patrick's seemed to change. Part of my duties there was to lock up all offices and public areas for the night and to patrol these areas during the night. It was while carrying out these duties that I began to sense that I was not alone in certain parts of the building. While walking along a corridor I could feel someone else in the corridor with me. On one occasion I heard what was the sound of footsteps behind me on a part of a corridor that I had just locked up. Having had an interesting paranormal past, these occurrences did not frighten or intimidate me in any way. One night while I was out on an external patrol I came across one of the more senior porters of the hospital. I asked him if he ever experienced anything strange in the hospital. I explained what I had felt while walking around the hospital and he told me that it was just the ghost of Jonathan Swift. I already knew of the connection between Swift and the hospital. On 19th October 1745 the venerable and sick Dean of St. Patrick's Cathedral in Dublin, and author of *Gulliver's Travels*, died leaving his entire estate derived from royalties of his writings including his great satirical work *Gulliver's Travels*, for the founding of the first hospital for the psychiatrically ill in Ireland. The hospital was granted a Royal Charter by George II on 8th August 1746. One of its earliest governors, a treasurer to the board and visiting state physician to the hospital was Dr Robert Emmet, father of the patriot. St. Patrick's hospital was built by architect George Semple following Dean Swift's detailed and painstaking instructions. It is now the oldest, purpose built psychiatric hospital continuously functioning on its original site in these islands, and one of the oldest in the world.

Jonathan Swift was born in Dublin on 30th November 1667, second child and only son of Jonathan Swift and Abigail Erick Swift. Jonathan Swift never knew his father because he died before Jonathan was born, so the young swift's education was arranged by other relatives. Jonathan graduated from Trinity College Dublin in 1686 and then went to England and found a job as secretary to Sir William Temple, and it was in Sir William's household that he met Esther (Stella) Johnson and became her tutor.

But when Sir William died in 1699, Jonathan was left scrambling for a job and eventually ended up with several small Church positions back in Ireland. He became a very fashionable satiric writer as far as Dublin society was concerned.

Gulliver's Travels was published in 1726 and though it has been labelled a children's book, it's also a great satire of the times. It shows Jonathan's desire to encourage people to read deeper and not take things for granted. In 1729, Swift wrote *A Modest Proposal*, supposedly written by an intelligent and objective "political arithmetician" who had carefully studied Ireland before making his proposal.

Swift died on 19th October 1745, aged 78. He hadn't been in a good frame of mind for some time. He managed to keep some of his sense of humour, and through his last will and testament he provided funds to establish somewhere around Dublin a hospital for "idiots and lunatics because no other nation wanted or needed it so much".

The life of St. Patrick's Hospital spans two and a half centuries of tumultuous social and political change in Ireland,

Even though Jonathan Swift never saw his dream of a hospital for "idiots and lunatics" become a reality while he was living, he is certainly keeping a close eye on it from the realms of the spirit world, for not only has his spirit been heard by myself but others have reported hearing and seeing it wandering its lonely corridors at night. Today the hospital is still owned by the Eastern Health Board and it is a training and administrate hospital with a new building to the rear still caring for the mentally ill of Dublin.

St Patrick's Hospital,
James Street, Dublin 8

Hellfire Club

Perched high on top of the Dublin mountains stands the Hellfire Club overlooking Dublin city from the south west at an altitude of 383m (1264ft). It is a foreboding ruined hunting lodge and folklore insists on telling us that it was, and still is, a site used for the practice of "Satanism", human sacrifice and other satanic occult activities, and yes, the Devil himself is reported to have made a brief appearance there at some unspecified time in the past. The story goes like this: *"a mysterious stranger seeks shelter on a stormy night and a card game ensues. A member of the household drops a card and sees it underneath the table. Bending down to retrieve the fallen card they glance across the under side of the table, but to their horror the otherwise affable and charming visitor has a cloven hoof; the mark of the Devil. The ensuing screams made the Devil aware of this discovery and he at once vanished in a thunder-clap, leaving a brimstone smell behind him".* It is interesting that this story also resembles a similar story attached to another of Ireland's most famous haunted houses Loftus Hall. Although the name Hellfire Club was founded at West Wycombe, England in 1741 by Sir Francis Dashwood the Earl of Rosse, it was Richard Parsons who in 1735 founded the Irish branch. The Irish Hellfire Club acquired for themselves the house built on Montpelier Hill southwest of Dublin by William Connolly, with members among his friends and colleagues. They met in the Eagle Tavern on Cork Hill in Dublin, but occasionally they met in the old shooting lodge outside Dublin which is now known as the Hellfire Club. It was at the time no more than a drinking and gambling club with all sorts of debauchery and prostitution. The members were mostly young lads from a high social background, who thought they could get away with lewd outlandish behaviour and were able buy themselves out of any sticky situation. They were privileged and well connected young men out to raise hell. Satanic rites are reported to have taken place within the walls of the club. The black magic element was something which the club liked to project about themselves whether or not it was true. Some of the reported satanic acts supposed to have happened there are one of a wandering priest who stumbled upon the club during a macabre satanic act and was forced to look on. The focus of attention was a huge black cat. When the cat broke free from his captors, the cleric grabbed it uttering an exorcism which tore the beast apart. A demon shot up from its corpse and hurtling through the roof it brought down the ceiling and scattered the assembly. Another time the club is said to have met the devil in the form of a "black man" in the lodge's dining room. After the death of its founder in 1741 the club became inactive but the cult continued, with the 2nd Earl of Rosse as its leader. The Hellfire Club is now a ruin without windows in any of the openings and the cold harsh wind of the Dublin mountains howls throughout the entire building. Because of its remote location there is no requirement to make a booking to visit the building, just the energy to climb to the top of the hill that it is located on.

Be advised if you are visiting the club to make sure you lock up your car well and do not leave any valuables in view. I would not recommend an investigation there. As you cannot take a car up to the club your vehicle will be a long distance from you in a remote location after dark. But if you do decide to visit, make sure a friend drops you off and picks you up at a pre-determined time. Stay as part of a large group and notify the local authorities of your activities.

Huntington Castle

In 1625 the 1st Lord Esmonde built Huntington Castle, replacing an earlier stronghold built in the 15th century. The castle was built on land originally owned by the O'Kavanaghs but granted to the Neterville family by Elizabeth 1 before being sold to Lord Esmonde. Huntington Castle has a spellbinding quality with its long dark creaking corridors, displaying suits of armour watching your every movement through the castle. Dusty family portraits hang on walls and books with cobwebs are stacked on shelves calling you to approach and be in awe of the titles. The old core of Huntington Castle is a tower house built between 1625 and 1630 by Laurence, first and last Lord Esmonde. The castle remained largely unaltered until 1849 when the property was inherited by Alexander Durdin, whose grand-uncle had married the two daughters and co-heirs of Sir John Esmonde, third Bart, as his two successive wives. Alexander Durdin's other changes to the castle were continued by his daughter Helen following her marriage in

1880 to Herbert Robertson, formerly Tory MP for Hackney South. Huntington was one of the first castles in Ireland to have electricity, and in order to satisfy local interest a light was kept burning on the front lawn so that the curious could come up and inspect it. Huntington is indeed a castle of character, filled with the spirits of the past. Perhaps the most interesting of all rooms is the dining-room which used to be the old hall of the castle. Its granite fireplace has the date 1625 inscribed on the keystone. To the right is a stained glass genealogical window made in 1870 by Powell which traces the family's lineage back to Lord Esmonde.

Huntington Castle has been home to the Durid-Roberts family for some 200 years. In the garden is an old yew tree walk that is reported to be 600 years old. It reminds me of the overhanging pathway of oak trees at Charleville Castle in Tullamore, Co. Offaly. It invites you in but something tells you not to. This is a castle where the extraordinary becomes the ordinary. Huntington Castle has an appeal of its own despite the presence of a dungeon, which was last used as late as 1921 when the castle was occupied by the IRA who were involved in a battle there. Huntington Castle is eerie and very much haunted, as is the yew walk with its intertwining branches forming a long and mysterious tunnel that leads to a monastery. Ghosts of monks have been seen walking from the tunnels on several occasions. In the garden the spirit of Lord Esmonde's first wife Lady Esmonde awaits the return of her caring husband. She has been seen sitting in the shadow of the Spy Bush day and night with a phantom white cat at her feet patiently looking out for her loved one. She can be seen combing her long hair by the moonlight and wailing in grief stricken anguish waiting for her husband and son to return from the war.

A soldier in ghost form has been known to knock on the door. He is thought to have lived in the castle in the 17th century having disguised himself in the uniform of the royalist to escape the Cromwellian forces. He was shot through the grille of the door in the uniform of the Royal opposition in the 17th century when his own men didn't recognize him.

Another spirit of Huntington Castle is that of Barbara St. Lege (1748-1820) who married into the family. A portrait of Barbara St. Lege still hangs on the wall in Huntington Castle and her spirit can be seen walking the corridors jangling her keys followed by the spirit of her maid Honour Byrne, who for some strange reason pauses to polish all the door handles with her hair. Yet another spirit, that of Bishop Leslie of Limerick, haunts the four poster room where he stayed when he lived at the castle. He has startled many guests who have woken to see him standing at the foot of the bed staring at them. The Bishop's face is also reported to appear in a portrait of a Spanish flower girl. This strange apparition has on occasions frightened guests through the years.

Huntington Castle to me is timeless and priceless. It has stood the test of time with dignity and pride.

Huntington Castle,
Clonegal,
Co. Carlow

Johnnie Fox's Pub

Johnnie Fox's Pub is world famous for being one of Dublin's oldest and highest pubs. Johnnie Fox's was established in 1798, the same year as the Irish uprising, and is located snugly in a small rural and rugged part of the Dublin mountains in Glencullen. Take the winding road from Dublin via Rathfarnham, then take the Enniskerry Road to Glencullen. This will take you through the breathtaking scenic and panoramic splendour of South Co. Dublin. When you step into Johnnie Fox's you step back in time, for little has changed within these walls since it was first built. Stepping into the dark porch you enter a long low yet cosy building that is like a museum to Ireland's past, for adorning the walls are old farm tools, flintlock guns and there is even a penny-farthing bike. A coffin carrier dating as far back as the 1840s (most likely used during the Irish Famine) does not look out of place among these curious objects. There are countless old pictures of Ireland's past, but most unusual of all the items that adorn the walls are the ashes of one of its patrons. These ashes were interned there at the request of the patron before he died, and as with Irish tradition a dying man's wishes are granted. During its history Johnnie Fox's had a great association with national politics. Daniel O'Connell was a frequent visitor to the pub and is believed to have held the first meeting of the Catholic Association while enjoying some fine ale here. Another one of Ireland's political leaders Michael Collins is reported to have set up an ammunitions factory in one of the outbuildings for the 1916 rising.

Johnnie Fox's Pub

Staff have reported that in the early mornings there is an eerie feeling about the place like someone else is there with them. Some visitors have asked the staff about the old gent sitting in the corner who seems to stare at nothing in particular, only to be told that it's simply the ghost. Staff say don't worry, he will be leaving soon and sure enough he would be gone the next time the visitor looked over. Other patrons have felt a tap on their shoulder, but when they turned around there was nobody there. Could this gentle tapping be the spirit of the gentleman whose ashes are interred within the walls of the pub? Could he be playing tricks on his old drinking buddies, or is it an old owner of the pub just popping by to say hello? Who is the old gent who sits alone staring into space then vanishes? We will never know. But one thing is for certain, when you visit Johnnie Fox's Pub you are greeted with a warm Irish welcome, great beer and fine food. But while you sit there enjoying your meal look over into the corner, you never know who you will see sitting there.

Johnnie Fox's Pub,
Glencullen,
Co. Dublin
Phone: 01 2955647
www.jfp.ie

Kilgobbin Castle

The Walsh family of Carrickinines, comrades in the protection of the Pale, later on settled on the lands of Kilgobbin. The Walsh family erected the castle. Amongst its successive occupants were, in 1482 Morris Walsh; in 1509 Pierce, son of Morris Walsh; in 1578 John Walsh; in 1599 Edmond Walsh; in 1615 Christopher Walsh; and in 1620 Patrick, *alias* Pierce Walsh and son of John Walsh. In his time a court was held by order of the Exchequer at Kilgobbin, and certain persons were found guilty of non-attendance by a jury composed of the Walsh's and their neighbours.

The lands of Balyofryn, on the dissolution of the religious houses, had come into the possession of the Corporation of Dublin, and in the reign of Queen Elizabeth we find Jacques Wingfield, the tenant of Stillorgan, holding them and covenanting to build a castle upon them.

Before the 1641 rebellion Sir Adam Loftus of

Rathfarnham took possession of Kilgobbin Castle and under him it was then occupied by one Matthew Talbot. Talbot became an officer in the Irish Army, and an unfortunate widow who lived near him on the lands of Murphystown relates in a deposition how he deprived her of all her possessions and how in the castle at Kilgobbin she besought his mother, "a woman not moved with compassion", to restore her a pittance to buy corn for her children.

In the following January, on the very same day as that on which Dundrum Castle was taken, a party of horsemen proceeded to the Castle of Kilgobbin. On their approach they came under a barrage of musket fire, one of the soldiers was mortally wounded and others were also wounded. Some prominent leaders of the Irish are said to have been in the castle at the time and to have afterwards escaped. Subsequently the castle was possessed by General Monk and was garrisoned, as well as Loughlinstown Castle, by his company.

After the establishment of the Commonwealth the castle became the residence of Dr. John Harding an ex-fellow of Trinity College, Dublin.

He was one of the greatest political leaders of his time. A native of Staffordshire England and graduate of Cambridge University, he was in 1637 imposed on Trinity College as an upholder of absolute monarchy. He died at Kilgobbin castle in 1665. About the middle of the 18th century Kilgobbin passed through the hands of various owners, including the Eustace's of Harristown, the McDonnells of Antrim, and Richard Nutley. Kilgobbin

Castle is now a sad shell of its former glory but it still holds a magical fascination in the paranormal world, for it is reported to be haunted by the ghost of a woman who is said to be related to the castle. Who she is no one knows, but people have reported hearing the rustling of chains and seeing the ghost of the old lady. Maybe she was imprisoned in the castle and now her spirit is still imprisoned within its walls, shackled and forever walking its now empty rooms.

Kilgobbin Castle is located on privately owned land in Stepaside, Co. Dublin.

Killakee House

Killakee House is nestled snugly in the Wicklow Mountains at the base of the Hellfire Club at Killakee Road, Rathfarnham. This romantic, typically Irish cottage presents an image of tranquilly, but behind its doors lies the reality of a turbulent and satanic past that seems to be a focus for violence and mysterious phenomena, perhaps stemming from the Hellfire Club's activities or the destruction of the cairn.

Constance Markievicz, the first woman elected to the House of Commons, resided at Killakee House. Markievicz took part in the Rising of 1916, and during her stay there a gun battle killed five members of the newly-formed IRA.

The 1960s saw the house become an arts centre, and it was this time which saw the dawning of the events for which Killakee is most famous. Upon moving to the house, the arts centre's employees heard legends from the locals of a huge black cat, dating to 1918. In 1968

Margaret O'Brien and her husband Nicholas purchased what was then a derelict building intending to turn it into an arts centre. During the renovation the many workmen living on the site soon grew used to eerie sounds and uncanny happenings. But when a large feline appeared mysteriously before them and suddenly vanished the builders became uneasy, thus the legend of the black cat of Killakee was born.

Margaret O'Brien did indeed see on several occasions some "big black animal". The first time she crossed its path, it was squatting on the flagstones of the hallway just glaring at her. Every door in the house was locked both before and after its sudden appearance and subsequent disappearance. But it was artist Tom McAssey who had the most famous sighting of the black cat of Killakee. After the front door had mysteriously unlocked itself, he saw a large black cat lying outside. McAssey said the cat seemed to speak to him, saying "You don't see me", but when he tried to lock the door the cat is reported to have said "Leave this door open".

Margaret O'Brien encountered many other ghostly phenomena at the house, many of them poltergeist-like in nature. She called in a Catholic priest to perform an exorcism, but to no avail. The haunting continued. In March 1968 Nicholas and two other men were working in a room of the house, when the temperature began to drop. Suddenly the door swung wide open and a hazy figure appeared in the darkness. Thinking that this was someone playing a joke he called out "Come in, I can see you". But all of them froze in sheer terror when the only reply was an angry growl. Not wanting to find out what was making the noise they fled the room slamming the door behind them. But then in October 1969 a group of actors staying there decided to hold a séance just for the fun of it, but this only brought the disturbances back. They also apparently made contact with the spirits of two nuns. A local medium visited the property and claimed that the phantoms were the unhappy spirits of two women who had assisted at satanic rituals held during the meetings of the notorious Hell Fire Club in the 18th century.

In July 1970 during some renovation to Killakee House, workers found a dwarfish skeleton buried under the kitchen floor. This discovery only gave more fuel to the legend associated with the Hellfire Club. In the grave with the dwarf was a brass statuette of a demon. The priest was called a second time and the body properly buried. The manifestations have stopped.

Killakee House,
Killakee Road,
Rathfarnham,
Dublin 16

Killula Castle

Killula Castle today is a sad reflection of its former glory. Standing proud on a hill top in Killula, Co. Westmeath, this once majestic house was the home of the Chapman family. Originally from England, the Chapman family obtained their land from their cousin Sir Walter Raleigh. The lands were confiscated from the Knights Hospitallers of St. John at Killula. Benjamin Chapman became a captain in Cromwell's army and was granted Killula Castle and lands. Killula Castle now became the ancestral home of the Chapman family.

The Chapman family, of whom the legendary Lawrence of Arabia is the most famous, lived in Killula at Clonmellon and Southill at Delvin. Cousins of Sir Walter Raleigh, the first Chapmans settled in Cork and Kerry. Thomas Chapman was born in 1848 and lived in Southill. He married a Rochford and they had four children. But his wife was a keen traveller and spent little time at home.

Discontented, he abandoned his home, his marriage and his name to live with his mistress Sarah Dunne in Wales. He then adopted the name Robert Lawrence. They had seven children, the most famous of whom was Thomas Edward, an intriguing and enigmatic figure who led the Arabs in World War I earning himself the title "Lawrence of Arabia".

Today, Killula is a spectacular ivy-clad ruin, and an obelisk monument on the grounds commemorates the Chapman relationship to Sir Walter Raleigh. It is also reported that this is the spot where he planted the first potato. Close to the rear entrance to the estate is Clonmellon Cemetery where the Chapman family graves may be seen. The present structure of Killula Castle was built in 1780 and was later converted into the romantic Gothic fantasy castle that we know today in 1830.

As you approach the ruins today you cannot but think of how it resembles a mystical castle from Camelot, how the many dark empty windows seem to draw your imagination into its dark eerie hollow empty rooms. As you enter the neglected decaying rooms you can almost feel your heart pounding within your chest as you anticipate someone popping out from behind one of the many crumbling walls.

But it's the strange occurrences at Killula Castle that remain a mystery. A white glowing spectre is said to wander its inner rooms and outer walls at night. No one has ever seen this apparition up close so its gender is unknown and there are several different accounts of who this is reported to be. Some say it's the spirit of the daughter of one of the former residents who met with a tragic accident within the castle, but nothing can be found in records to substantiate any daughter meeting a tragic death. Others say it is the spirit of an 18th century Stewart of the castle who was haunted by the demons that come with drink. But no matter who it is we cannot discount the many sightings of this glowing spirit that walks the grounds of Killula Castle.

Killula Castle,
Killula,
Co. Westmeath

Kilmainham Gaol

The foundations of the gaol were laid in 1786 when the Dublin authorities, fearing a spread of French revolutionary ideas would infect this county, carried out further expansions to the original plans for the gaol and delayed the official opening. The gaol was soon filled with political prisoners over a period lasting nearly 130 years. Among the first to arrive were Henry Joy McCracken and many of his United Irish Men associates of 1798. But the rebels of 1798 were soon followed by the supporters of Robert Emmet's revolt. The Fenian rising of 1867 and the activities of the land league in the 1880s led to more people being detained. Kilmainham Gaol was indeed a busy place in Irish history. Life inside the gaol was not easy: cold damp cells and hard labour were the order of the day. But not all of Kilmainham Gaol's political prisoners left its thick walls. Some of Ireland's most famous political leaders met their death inside the gaol.

The leader of the 1798 rebellion, Wolfe Tone committed suicide before he could be executed. Thomas Francis Meagher, leader of the rebellion in 1848, and Charles Stewart Parnell, leader of the rebellion in 1867,

Kilmainham Gaol

were executed. The rebellion of 1916 led to fourteen of its leaders being executed within the gaol. These were: James Connolly, Seán Mac Diarmada, Thomas J. Clarke, P.H. Pearse, Willie Pearse, Eamonn Ceannt, Cornelius 'Con'

Kilmainham Gaol

Colbert, Seán Heuston, Michael Mallin, Thomas MacDonagh, Edward Daly, Michael O'Hanrahan, John MacBride and Joseph Plunkett, who were all executed in the period 3rd-12th May 1916.

But Kilmaimham Gaol did have a brief joyous moment for one of its political prisoners. After his surrender in the 1916 rebellion Joseph Plunkett was arrested and imprisoned in the gaol. Just hours before his execution on 4th May 1916 he was allowed to marry his sweetheart Grace Gifford. They were married in the small chapel within the prison walls, the marriage was witnessed by prison guards. Shortly after the sermon Joseph Plunkett was taken out to

175

the execution yard and executed for his part in the Easter Rising.

Do the spirits of Ireland's leaders still roam the corridors of Kilmainham Gaol today? Heavy footsteps along the empty corridors and forceful winds are just some of the regular reported experiences by visitors to the gaol today. I have visited the gaol many times and have assisted a television company to carry out a investigation into the science of fear, and have found its dark lonely corridors threatening and intimidating to the extent that you would often look behind you just to make sure you are alone.

Kilmainham Gaol is a national monument and museum and can be visited most of the year. Tours run daily between 9am and 5pm.

Kilmainham Gaol,
Inchicore,
Dublin 8
Phone: 01 4535984

Kinnitty Castle

Nestling at the foothills of the Slieve Bloom mountains is Kinnity Castle as majestic as its long and turbulent history. The first stronghold that was built on the site was destroyed in 1209 and rebuilt by the Normans in 1213. During this period an Augustinian Abbey was established near the castle of which the famous High Cross and Abbey walls still remain on the estate today. Later the Normans were driven out by the powerful Gaelic clan, the O'Carrolls.

In 1630 one of their line, William O'Carroll, built a new castle in close proximity to the old Abbey. This was confiscated in 1641 by the English forces as part of the plantation of Offaly.

In 1664 the estate passed to Colonel Thomas Winter as a reward for his military service. It remained within his family for another 200 years till one of his descendents sold it to the Bernard family. It was in 1811 that Lady Catherine Hutchinson, wife of Thomas Bernard,

Kinnitty Castle

commissioned the present castle to be built. In 1922, as with many stately homes in Ireland, the Castle was burned down by Republican forces. Kinnitty Castle was rebuilt in 1928 by the Bernard family and they lived there until 1946 when the castle was sold to Lord Decies who in turn sold it to the State in 1951. The State retained ownership until it was purchased by the Ryan family in 1994 who transformed it into a luxurious thirty-seven bedroom hotel. With Kinnitty Castle's long and turbulent history inevitably comes a ghostly presence.

The most famous ghost at Kinnitty Castle is that of a very friendly monk who is reported to be very tall and always appears to be dressed in black. His presence is mostly felt in The Great Hall of The O'Carrolls. This is because the monks have been here since 1100. He always

178

seems to enjoy overseeing weddings and conferences, as he loves the laughs and fun that people have. He would be the kind of spirit that would put himself between a bride and groom just for a laugh. But there is a more serious side to this playful monk as it seems he also has the ability to predict and foresee the future. He then passes his messages on through members of staff. It is reported that everything that he predicts comes true. He is also very fond of Con Ryan and always looks over him.

Many members of staff and guests, because they too have either seen him or felt his presence, believe in the monk. Kinnitty Castle is today a top class hotel open to guests all year round. So why not stay a night there – you might just be joined by one of its oldest guests for late night supper.

Kinnitty Castle,
Kinnitty,
Birr,
Co. Offaly
Phone: 0509 37318

Loftus Hall

Loftus Hall stands proud on Hook Peninsula. It was built by the 4th Marquis of Ely in 1870-1871 on the ruins of Redmond Hall which had existed since 1350. Redmond Hall became the property of the Loftus family in 1666 and became known as Loftus Hall thereafter. It is necessary, however, to go back a generation to his uncle, Henry the Earl of Ely who was an Irish MP 1747-1769. He was the first head of the family to establish a separate Loftus party in the Irish House of Commons comprised of at least eight MPs and was thus a major grouping in the parliament.

Henry the Earl of Ely died with no surviving family in 1783 and with this his peerages became extinct. The heir to all his estates was his sister's son Charles Tottenham, who assumed the name of Loftus and began the process of using his electoral interest to secure the recreation of the family honours. He was initially undecided about the merits of the Act of Union. However, during the summer of 1799 he and his political following decided to back the measure. His support and loyalty were rewarded by his promotion to the marquis and a barony in 1801. The Duke of Portland, the British Home Secretary, wrote to Marquis Cornwallis, Lord Lieutenant of Ireland, that if any marquis were created that it should be confined to Lord Ely whose influence is so extensive and has of late been so usefully employed.

It was here in this famous house that the "ghost of Loftus Hall" was born, the story originating in the middle of the 18th century. The story is that one cold rainy night the family of the house were sitting in the parlour playing card games. During the game they heard a loud knock on the front door. A man on horseback was standing at the door and asked them if he could stay the night because of the bad weather outside. The family agreed having taken pity on the man. He was invited in and joined in on the card game with the family. During the game one of the daughters of the family (who was about eighteen at the time) dropped a card under the table. As she bent down to pick it up she saw the man's feet which were in fact cloven hooves: the sign of the Devil. The girl screamed and the man leapt up and shot through the roof in a puff of smoke leaving behind a large hole. The family called on Father Thomas Broaders the local Catholic priest telling him the story. He got permission to exorcise the house. His powers and the power of his faith worked. Fr. Broaders later became a famous parish priest of the surrounding area because of this incident. And later became parish priest of the united parishes of the Hook for almost fifty years.

182

When Father Broaders died in January 1773 his tomb in Horetown Cemetery has the following epitaph inscribed on it.

> "Here lies the body of Thomas Broaders
> who did good and prayed for all
> and who banished the devil from Loftus hall"

Sadly the Loftus Hall in which this ghostly happening took place was destroyed in a fire and levelled to the ground in 1871. The present mansion stands on 70 acres and with five reception rooms and twenty-two bedrooms was occupied by the Benedictines from 1917 to 1935 and then by the Rossminians from 1937 until 1983. Loftus Hall is now a ruin and a sad shadow of its former glory but is still private property. You may wish to pop along to view Loftus Hall from the roadside.

Loftus Hall,
Hook Head,
Co. Wexford.

Malahide Castle

Malahide Castle is probably the most distinguished of all the Irish castles. It has without question endured the longest continuous occupation by far, for the Talbots reigned within the castle for 791 years. The Talbot family began their reign in 1185 and ended it in 1976 despite a short interlude from 1649 to 1660 while Cromwell marched through Ireland. The lands and harbour of Malahide were granted to Richard Talbot in 1185, one of the knights who arrived in Ireland with Henry II in 1174. The history of the Talbot family is recorded in the Great Hall where portraits of generations of the family tell a story of Ireland's stormy and bloody history. At the heart of this medieval castle is the Oak Room accessed by way of a winding stone staircase and lit by five Gothic windows which were added in 1820 when the room was enlarged. The room is lined with carved oak from floor to ceiling, now black with age and polished. Once you step into the

Malahide Castle

oak room you feel yourself stepping back in time as nothing seems to have changed since it was first built. One of the more poignant legends of Malahide Castle concerns the morning of the Battle of the Boyne in 1690, when fourteen members of the family headed by Dick Talbot (or fighting Dick as he was commonly known) sat down to breakfast together in this room, prior to joining the Catholic forces of King James. Fourteen members of the Talbot family marched out to battle on this fateful morning never to return as all were dead by nightfall. A lot of stately homes and castles in Ireland have a resident ghost or one that comes in visitation but Malahide Castle has five that frequent its majestic rooms. The first I will introduce to you is that of young Lord Galtrim.

Lord Galtrim was the son of Sir Walter Hussey who in the 15th century was killed in battle on his wedding day. This spirit of Lord Galtrim is reported to wander through the castle at night grasping the spear wound in his side that he received in battle and uttering dreadful groans. His spirit is supposed to haunt the castle in resentment towards his young bride, who married his rival immediately after he had given up his life and passed into the realms of the spirit world in defence of her honour and happiness.

The second reported spirit is that of the Lady Maud Plunkett who seemingly does not appear as she did on the day of her marriage to Lord Galtrim, but as she looked when she married her third husband the Lord Chief Justice. At this time she had become notorious as an unequalled virago and in her ghostly appearances is reported to be chasing her husband through the corridors of the Castle.

The third ghost is that of the Chief Justice himself who merely appears to furnish his spectral spouse with an opportunity of a little light-hearted chasing through the castle and some nocturnal exercise.

The fourth spirit is that of Miles Corbett. Miles was the Roundhead to whom Cromwell gave the castle and property during his protectorate. At the Restoration Miles Corbett was deprived of his property and made to pay the penalty of the many crimes he had committed during his occupancy, including the desecration of the chapel of the old abbey near the castle. When the monarchy was restored in 1660 Miles Corbett's life, like all those who had signed Charles's death warrant, was forfeit. He fled to the continent but was eventually captured at Delft. He was brought back to England, charged for his crimes and sentenced to be hanged, drawn and quartered with two other regicides at Tyburn on 19th April 1662. But strangely, when his ghost first appears it seems to be a perfectly whole soldier in full armour, but then seemingly falls into four pieces before the eyes of anyone who has the unpleasant experience of meeting him.

The fifth and last spirit is my favourite and has a

Graves, Malahide Castle

188

certain amount of pathos. In the 16th century as befitted a family of importance the Talbots always had a jester among their retinue of attendants. One of these jesters was "Puck". Puck fell in love with a kinswoman of Lady Elenora Fitzgerald who was detained at the castle at the pleasure of Henry VIII because of her rebel tendencies. On a snowy December night Puck the jester was found lying at the base of the walls of the castle stabbed through the heart, a tragic figure in his gay jester suit and cap and bells. Before he died he swore an oath that he would haunt the castle until a master reigned who chose a bride from the people, but would harm no one if a male Talbot slept under the roof. Puck's last appearance was reported during the sale of the contents of the Castle in May 1976. His dwarfed figure makes its appearance in many photographs of the castle. He is reported to be seen at his own special door known as Puck's door. I have visited Malahide Castle on many occasions and always find its splendour inspiring. Unfortunately none of its five spirits have graced me with their presence, but one keeps on hoping.

Malahide Castle is owned and run by Fingal County Council and is open to the public all year round.

Malahide Castle,
Malahide,
Co. Dublin

Phone: 01 8462184

Marsh's Library

Marsh's Library was established by Archbishop Marsh in 1701 and was furnished with his own collection of books and those he purchased from Edward Stillingfleet. The collection of Dr. Elias Bouhéreau, the first librarian of Marsh's Library, was also added during this time. A fourth major collection was bequeathed in 1745 by John Stearne, Bishop of Clogher. More books were added over the years and at present the library houses over 25,000 books including 80 incunabula and 5000 books printed in England before 1700. Marsh's Library is one of the few 18th century buildings in Dublin that is still used for its original purpose. The library was formally incorporated in 1707 by an Act of Parliament called *"An Act for settling and preserving a public library for ever"*. The interior of the library resembles the inside of a church with its beautiful dark oak bookcases each with its own carved and lettered gables, topped by a mitre. The three elegant wired alcoves or "cages", where the readers were locked with rare books to prevent them from stealing them, has remained unchanged today since it was built over 300 years ago.

Narcissus Marsh was born in Wiltshire, England in 1638. His father was William Marsh and his mother, Grace Colburn. Narcissus Marsh was the youngest of a family of three brothers and two sisters.

Marsh was educated in Oxford, England. He was ordained in 1662 and was sent to Ireland as Provost of Trinity College, Dublin in 1679. He first got the idea of setting up a public library during his time as Provost of Trinity College having observed how difficult it was to use the library there. He was appointed successively Bishop of Ferns and Leighlin in 1683, Archbishop of Cashel in 1691, Archbishop of Dublin in 1694 and Primate of Armagh in 1703.

In May 1700 Marsh wrote a letter to his dear friend Dr. Thomas Smith in England. In this letter he explains that he intends on building a public library in Dublin and asks for Dr. Smith's assistance in "recommending him choice books". He also explains that although the Archbishop's house, St. Sepulchre's where he lived "may well be called a Palace for the stateliness of all the public rooms of reception, (it) has no chapel or library, belonging to it, or even any convenient room to hold an ordinary study of books, so that mine lay dispersed in three distant rooms".

During Marsh's time as an Archbishop of Dublin he lived as an old bachelor in the Palace of St. Sepulchre. There he made arrangements for his niece, the young

Grace Marsh, to look after his housekeeping for him. Grace was only nineteen and young at heart and found the life of an Archbishop strict and the discipline rather depressing. In Marsh's Diary of 1695 there is an entry for the 10th September, "This evening between eight and nine of the clock at night my niece Grace Marsh (not having the fear of God before her eyes) stole privately out of my house at St. Sepulchre's and (as is reported) was that night married to Chas, Proby vicar of Castleknock in a Tavern and was bedded there with him – Lord consider my

Marsh's Library

affliction". Narcissus Marsh died in 1713 and is buried just outside his library, in the grounds of St Patrick's Cathedral. His niece Grace Marsh lived to be 85 years old and was buried in the same tomb with her uncle, the Archbishop. This tale of the elopement of Marsh's niece gave fuel to the story of the ghost of Marsh Library. The story goes that Grace regretted upsetting her uncle and left him a letter hidden in one of his books explaining what she could not tell him to his face. Marsh never found the letter and it is reported that his ghost haunts the library searching through the books for Grace's letter. The figure of an elderly man has been seen on several occasions in the inner gallery of the library searching through volumes of books that belonged to Narcissus Marsh. Hence it is generally taken for granted that this is the spirit of the Archbishop still searching for his niece's letter. I became intrigued by this story when I read about it in a book called *Irish Ghosts* by John J Dunne. I have visited the Library and have sat quietly among the thousands of books silently waiting for the spirit of Marsh to make an appearance, but nothing has happened. I enquired of the staff if any of them had ever seen the spirit of Marsh. They have not, but they like to think that his spirit still visits the library.

Marsh's Library,
St Patrick's Close,
Dublin 8,
Ireland

Phone: 01 4543511

Newbay House

In the 1400's a castle once stood on this land were Newbay House now stands. The French family, previous owners of Newbay House, founded the Canadian Mounties. George Arthur French was born in June 1842, the eldest son of John French. In his youth he gained entrance to the Royal Military Academy in Sandhurst, England. Having served in the various ranks, he was appointed to the Royal Artillery.

Following a request from the Canadian Government, George Arthur French was despatched to Canada where he became Inspector of Artillery. He was later appointed head of the school of Gunnery in Kingston.

Sir John MacDonald, the then prime minister of Canada, was in the process of setting up a Canadian Police Force to maintain law and order in the "Wild West". This mounted police was to be modelled on the Royal Irish Constabulary. Another member of the French family was appointed first commander of the North West Mounted Rifle in 1873 by the Canadian prime minister. He presided over the force as Lieutenant Colonel George French. The force changed its name to the North West Mounted Police and subsequently took the title of the Royal Canadian Mounted Police, better known as the Mounties.

For sixteen years his brother, John French, served in various military establishments before he joined the North West Mounted Police. He received many honours for his first rate horsemanship and headed up a battalion of mounted police in a rebellion. His troops were known as "French's Scouts" and French distinguished himself with many acts of bravery. However, he died in combat and French's Scouts which he founded, was disbanded.

George Arthur French attained the rank of Major General in the Canadian Police Force and was knighted in 1902. He died in 1921 and his funeral was attended by King George V. The last heir married a Canadian and settled in Canada, selling Newbay House to Paul and Min Drum.

Newbay House is a typical late Georgian country house set in 25 acres of gardens and parklands. Beyond a high wall in the garden is an ancient stable yard with Elizabethan buildings, said to be haunted by the ghost of a former owner, who was piked to death by insurrectionists in 1798. Open peat and log fires welcome arriving guests, and the house is decorated with stripped pine furniture. There are huge trees, lawns and bright flowerbeds in the garden. There is a pond with wild ducks and moorhens, and a peacock which strolls grandly about and poses on the porch above the kitchen door. Now restored and refurbished by Des Mullen and Joan Coyle, there are 25 acres of gardens and parkland and the house is close to beautiful beaches and many archaeological sites. Newbay House to me is a magical building with an intriguing paranormal history. The gardens are reported to be haunted by the ghost of Col. French after he was killed by insurgents during the 1798 rebellion. Within the house the bridal suite is the hub of activity. Staff have reported voices and the sensation of cobwebs on people's faces and spine-chilling cold shivers. Black moving blurs have been witnessed on a large mirror in the bridal suite.

Two staff members approached the bridal suite one day. Knowing that there were no guests in the house they knocked on the door anyway and upon doing this all of the lights in the room came on. This could be seen through the cracks in the closed door. Another staff member, while standing outside, saw someone standing at the bridal suite window only to discover later on that there had in fact been nobody in the room that night. On a separate occasion while the house was empty two staff members were walking up the corridor to a bedroom. When they came back down the corridor there was a bag filled with linen sitting in the middle of the corridor. It had not been there before. Before Newbay opened to the public a woman had lived alone there. She told of awaking one night feeling extremely cold as her dog stood barking and growling at an empty space.

Footsteps can often be heard upstairs in the house when there is nobody else in residence. With all this activity Newbay is a must to visit.

Newbay Country House,
Newbay, Co. Wexford

Phone: 053 22779

Portlick Castle

Portlick Castle is built on the outskirts of Glasson in Co. Westmeath. It is one of the few Medieval castles in Ireland that has always been lived in.

Built by the Norman family of De Lion in 1185 under the charter of King John, the family were devout Catholics who fought in the Irish rebellion. Although banished for a time to Connaught by Cromwell they did not leave their home for good, returning in 1696.

The De Lions later became known as the Dillions who were supporters of King James during the Jacobean and Williamite wars. With the new monarch of King William, Dillion decided to grant the property to someone more loyal than himself, a privy councillor of Ireland named Thomas Keightly.

Keightly promptly sold his new home to William Palmer of Dublin. The price tag was £365, £1 for every acre the castle was built on. In 1703 Palmer then sold the castle to the Rev. Robert Smyth for £885. The Smyths like the Dillions before them were long-term and colourful owners. As early as 1782 the Smyths' reign there looked destined to come to an end. The Rev. Robert Smyth's son, Ralph, had just died and it was generally assumed that as a bachelor he had no heirs. Jane Rogerson, Ralph's sister, prepared to take over her inheritance to the castle. As was to be expected, some distant relatives emerged and began to lay claim to Portlick Castle, insisting that they were the true and rightful heirs. The future ownership of the castle was decided, however, when a local woman came forward. Maggie Gerrily presented her son, Robert, as Ralph's secret child and heir. A local clergyman confirmed the story and the Smyth name was secured at Portlick once more.

In 1812 the grand-daughter of the second Robert Smyth, Frideswide Smyth, fell in love and began courting a young naval officer by the name of Richard Brydges Beechey. Beechey was at the time assisting in the preparation of the Admiralty Chart of the nearby Lough Ree. It is because of his romantic relationship with Frideswide, it is said, that the Bay at Portlick received a lot more attention in this report than other areas. The two love birds later married and their son, RB Beechey, became known as one of Ireland's top three marine painters.

Sadly for Portlick Castle a large fire gutted part of the castle in 1861. This fire destroyed much of the Smyth family treasures including portraits and furnishings.

The last Smyth to live in Portlick was Harriet, the great great grand-daughter of the second Robert Smyth. Her stepson was killed in World War II and her husband, Norman Wallard Simpson, died in 1955.

In a thousand years of history, Portlick Castle has witnessed civil war, family disputes, devastating fire and the natural ravages of time, but despite all this it is still as impressive and as well preserved as ever. Now no longer the family seat of the Smyths, Portlick Castle has entered a new phase as a country retreat to escape from the hustle and bustle of everyday life. Portlick Castle is luxuriously decorated. As you enter through the large entrance hall you are greeted by the main stairway, a large drawing room with beautiful fireplace, a library and minstrel's gallery with dumbwaiter connection to the kitchen. The main tower links to the Victorian wing, the 15th century floor and the minstrel's gallery. A terrace overlooks the gardens and Lough. Portlick, like a lot of castles in Ireland, has its resident ghosts.

There is the ghost of a lady in old-fashioned dress with a bun in her hair in the upstairs office, and the sighting of only the legs and arms of a man climbing the back stairs. In the great room up on the balcony there are reports of a shadow that moves from one doorway to the centre of the room and then paces back and forth. He then leans on the railings and watches whoever is in the room below. Ghostly voices have also been heard within the walls of Portlick Castle.

Portlick Castle,
Glasson,
Co. Westmeath

Rathfarnham Castle

The original Rathfarnham Castle was an Anglo-Norman castle built to defend the Pale from hording Irish clans from the nearby Wicklow mountains. The Baltinglass family were its owners until 1583 when the castle was confiscated for their involvement in the Desmond Rebellions. The building we know today as Rathfarnham Castle was designed by James Stewart and William Chambers and it is believed that the castle was built for Archbishop Loftus. It was built around 1583, the same year as the original castle was confiscated from the Baltinglass family.

As you walk through the front door you come into a low-ceilinged entrance half flagged in limestone. The walls are adorned with six medallions of classic heads, some of them of Cleopatra with the famous asp and Lucreza with a dagger. Upstairs in the massive ballroom the Venetian window that is flanked with pairs of Corinthian pillars is only the introduction to this castle's beauty. Throughout its history the castle passed through many families, but the most important family to reside within its walls was the Loftus family. Its first owner Archbishop Loftus left the castle to his son Dudley. Dudley continued the family tradition and passed it onto his son Adam in 1616. But it was during Adam's reign in the castle that it came under siege during the 1641 rebellion. Adam opposed the treaty of cessation in order to stop the fighting and as a result he was imprisoned in Dublin Castle. The British Civil War began in 1642 and it is believed that Cromwell's Parliamentary troops were stationed at the castle. It has also been reported that Cromwell held council there before going to Wexford and Drogheda to kill the native Irish.

Adam Loftus sided with the Parliamentarians and was killed at the siege of Limerick in 1651.

After the British Civil War the Loftus family retained ownership of the castle. And in 1659 Dr. Dudley Loftus, the great grandson of Archbishop Loftus, took over the castle. During his lifetime Dudley held the posts of Commissioner of Revenue, Judge Admiralty, Master in Chancery, M.P for Kildare and Wicklow and M.P for Bannow and Fethard. His body is laid to rest in St. Patrick's Cathedral. The castle was passed down the centuries to the descendants of Dr. Dudley Loftus until it came into the hands of Philip Wharton. This young man spent his inheritance recklessly and incurred massive gambling debts and in 1724 the castle was then sold to

William Connolly. Connolly was a famous politician and a speaker in the House of Commons. Connolly was responsible for the building of the Hell Fire Club, one of many famous hell fire clubs within England and Ireland. The Castle remained in the hands of the Connolly family until 1742 when it was then sold to Bishop Hoadley. It stayed in the Hoadley family until 1763. The castle became the property of the Loftus family again and they constructed another entrance for the castle in the form of a Roman triumphal arch. This entrance can still be seen today from the Dodder Park Road.

It was in 1812 that the Loftus family finally said goodbye to the castle for the last time and moved to Loftus Hall, Co. Wexford. The castle then went through many different families such as the Ropers (1812-1852) and the Blackburn family (1852-1912). Bailey and Gibson acquired the castle in 1912 and built a golf course on its land. In 1913 the Jesuits bought the castle and the remaining land.

The castle was then sold to Delaware Properties in 1985 and faced demolition. But after immense public pressure to save the building the state purchased it in 1987, making it a national monument. But the most chilling story about Rathfarnham Castle is that of a skeleton. It was found in a room off the ballroom known as the octagonal room. The skeleton was found in a hollow in the walls in 1880. It is ascertained that she was there for over 130 years locked into a secret compartment in the room during a ball. Her two suitors were arguing over her love so they decided to sort out their differences in the traditional gentlemanly way, by having a duel. The successor would then rescue the fair maiden from the wall. But as bad luck had it for the fair maiden, both of her brave suitors died in the duel, one from drowning and the other from his wounds. As with all duels the whole affair was conducted in secret, so no one knew of the beautiful maiden who was concealed within the hollow wall and left there entombed where she died. The owner of the castle, a Mrs Blackburne, had the corpse's silk dress made into cushions. The fair maiden is reported to haunt the castle, especially the octagonal room, probably still waiting to be rescued by her brave romantic suitors.

Rathfarnham Castle,
Rathfarnham,
Dublin 14

Phone: 01 493 9462

Ross Castle, Co. Meath

Situated amidst majestic trees in the tranquil countryside of Co. Meath and the Cavan border, Ross Castle commands magnificent views of Lough Sheelig.

The Castle of Ross was originally built by Richard de Nugent the 12th Baron of Delvin in the 1533. The tower was completed by him in 1537. The great hall and further extensions were finished by his grandson and successor, Richard the 13th Baron by 1539.

The original de Nugents left France to join Norman William in the invasion of England in 1066. Among the names of the principal men who took part in the Norman Welsh invasion of Ireland (1169-1172) are to be found those of Gilbert de Nugent.

The celebrated Hugh de Lacy who had been granted the greater part of the County of Meath, had come to rely so much on the young Gilbert, that he gave him the hand of his only sister Rose in marriage. As a dowry he bestowed upon them the Barony of Delvin. De Lacy encouraged the building of strong castles for purposes of defense against the native owners from whom these lands had been taken.

In the centuries following, the de Nugents were always "King's Men". They never would forget that all they owned had been granted them by the power of the larger island across the Irish sea. They did their utmost to maintain the English foothold in the new colony; and while this was no simple task, they spread out and added to their own territory. By the 15th century they were in possession of lands as far north as the shores of Lough Sheelin on the Breffni border.

Built in the 16th century, the tower of Ross Castle was used by the celebrated Myles O'Reilly, otherwise known as "The Slasher", the night before being killed by Cromwell's troops at the battle of the bridge of Finea in 1644. It was also the scene of the tragic love story of Orwin and Sabrina in 1536. The Lord of Delvin, Richard Nugent, had a daughter Sabrina. Sabrina was born with a heart problem but grew up to be a beautiful young woman. Like all well kept daughters of an English lord she would be left on her own while the lord of the manor was away on business. To keep herself busy Sabrina would go out walking around Ross Castle whiling her spare time away. Usually, she would have some governesses with her but now and again she would get away without being watched.

One of these days she was walking along the bridge that was the border of her father's kingdom, when she met a handsome young man. They got chatting and promised at their parting that they would meet up again. More and more Sabrina would sneak out to see Orwin. Orwin was the son of an Irish lord. Meetings like this were unheard of around Ross Castle, but now that they had fallen in love they couldn't help but start talking about what would happen to their love knowing that they could never be married.

Sabrina and Orwin decided to elope, but on the fateful day they wanted to say goodbye to the land where they had grown up. So they went out in a boat onto Lough Sheelin. Unfortunately, a storm blew up on the lake. The boat overturned and Orwin hit his head and died instantly. Sabrina was thrown out of the boat and was rescued by onlookers who watched this tragic incident unfold. They brought her back to the castle but she didn't waken for three days. When she awoke everyone was asleep around her. She went for a walk and found Orwin, who was laid out in the chapel on the grounds of Ross Castle. Sabrina died shortly after that, probably from a broken heart. There have been many sightings of the lovers since this by guests of the castle.

The castle later fell into disrepair and was restored in 1864 by Anna Maria O'Reilly, a lineal descendant of Myles O'Reilly. Richard Nugent was also known as the "Black Baron" and was infamous for hanging both men and women alike, giving his name to a field on the estate known locally as "the hangman's hollow". The castle has a reputation for hauntings, and previous guests have labelled rooms such as "The Cave" in the tower and the "Whisper Room" found on the ground floor. Activity such as screaming is heard in the large rear wing room known as

"The Scream Room", footsteps, doors opening, voices and shadows are seen and heard throughout the castle.

Ross Castle has both self catering, housekeeping suites and B&B rooms available.

Ross Castle,
Mountnugent,
Co. Meath
Phone: 049 8540237

The Shelbourne Hotel

In 1824 Martin Burke founded The Shelbourne Hotel on St. Stephen's Green in Dublin. Burke was an Irish Catholic entrepreneur from South Tipperary who decided that what Dublin needed was a quality hotel for the cream of society.

Martin Burke found a collection of fashionable townhouses at numbers 27, 28 and 29 St. Stephens Green. With a down payment of £1000, a further £2000 to be paid at a later date plus a yearly rent of £300, he acquired the houses and converted them into a grand hotel fit for the wealthy.

Burke and his heirs were granted the leasehold for 150 years and thus The Shelbourne Hotel was born. In 1825 gas lighting was added to the hotel. In 1863 Martin Burke died and The Shelbourne Hotel was sold to a consortium of hoteliers, namely Jury, Cotton and Goodman. By 1867, a refit of The Shelbourne was completed, with a brand new facade and interior. Accommodation and facilities included

Coffee Room, Ladies Coffee Room, Table d'Hote Room, Reading Room, Smoking Room, Billiards Room, Hair-dressing Room and Telegraph Office. Also 15 bedrooms with bathrooms and 24 first class sitting rooms arranged en suite. In 1886 the new owners purchased No 32 St. Stephen's Green for £3,200 further extending the hotel. From 1906 till 1913 the hotel enjoyed great success with its Edwardian cliental and was further enhanced with a telephone and a lift. With the industrial revolution now in full swing clients started to arrive by car and by tram. The summer of 1912 saw a great influx of visitors from afar: USA, Japan, Iceland and Australia.

In 1914 the hotel had several German staff and these were interned as the Shelbourne became a hub of much military activity. The Easter Rising of 1916 did not even stop afternoon tea for the cliental of the hotel. Regardless of rebellion on the streets of Dublin, and the gun battle raging just the other side of the Green at the Royal College of Surgeons, the hotel performed to a full drawing room of ladies keen to show off their new hats. It was only when a stray sniper's bullet managed to take off the heads of some roses pinned to one of the patron's hats that guests were forced to move from the Lounge to the Reading Room for safety.

In 1922 British rule ended and Ireland needed a new constitution, and in room 112 of the Shelbourne the constitution for the new Irish Free State was drafted, under the chairmanship of Michael Collins. The room is now called The Constitution Suite.

1960 saw another dramatic change for The Shelbourne

Hotel as it changed hands and became part of the Trusthouse Forte Group, undergoing a £7m restoration programme. Over the next few years the Shelbourne Hotel changed hands several times. In 1997 The Shelbourne celebrated its 175th Anniversary with a Gala Event in the Great Room.

It is room number 526 that is of interest from a paranormal point of view. It has been reported that back in 1965 when a couple from America stayed in this room strange happenings took place. On 16th August 1965 while the couple were trying to sleep, they heard what they thought was a cat but as they listened more closely they realised that it was a young girl crying. It is also reported that the woman who was staying in the room that night was in fact psychic and made contact with the crying spirit. The psychic called out 'Who is here with us? Why are you crying?' 'I am frightened' came the reply from a young girl's voice. 'Don't be frightened, come closer' she beckoned to the spirit. With that they felt the sensation of a child climb onto the bed. They asked 'Who are you?'. 'I am Mary Mires' came the reply. 'How old are you Mary?' they asked. 'Six' came the reply. They also asked for the names of her parents; Timothy and Anne were the answers. They also discovered that the little spirit girl had a sister Sophie. It turned out that this room was not part of the original hotel but added afterwards. It also turned out that the spirit of little Mary was the spirit of a young child that lived in this part of the building when it was a private house and had in fact been the nursery. They tried to help little Mary Mires to cross over to the light but she was too frightened and it is reported that her little spirit still makes itself known to guests of one of Dublin's finest hotels.

The Shelbourne Hotel,
27 Stephen's Green,
Dublin 2,

Phone: 01 663 4500

St. Michan's Church

Founded around 1095 by the Danish colony in Oxmanstown and located near the Four Courts, St. Michan's is one of Dublin's more unusual attractions. Named after a Danish Bishop, it was for 500 years the only parish church on Dublin's north side of the River Liffey. The present building of St. Michan's dates from about 1685 when it was rebuilt to accommodate a more prosperous congregation that was gathered by Sir Humphrey Jervis.

From its founding until the mid 16th century monks from Christ Church Cathedral served the congregation of the church. Then in 1547 it became a part of Christ Church Cathedral with the Presenter of the Cathedral in charge of the parish. In 1870 the Church of Ireland was disestablished and disavowed, meaning it was no longer connected with the state and became a self-governing body. At this time the parish was separated from the Cathedral after which it became part of the Christ Church group of parishes.

Some historians believe the church may have been designed by Sir William Robinson, Ireland's Surveyor General (1645-1712).

In addition to the rebuilding in 1685, the church underwent extensive repair in 1828. During the war of independence in 1922 when rebel forces clashed at the Four Courts the constant shelling of the Four Courts, and the bad aim of the troops meant the roof of St. Michan's suffered damage and the east window was shattered and repaired with plain glass. In 1958 the present window was added, moved from St. Matthias's Church on Adelaide Road.

The organ at St. Michan's is one of the oldest in the country still in use. It is believed that George F. Handel played it when composing *The Messiah*. A panel on the organ gallery, carved from a single block of wood, portrays a series of musical instruments in high relief.

The main attraction at St Michan's, however, lies in the vaults underneath the church, where access is reached by a narrow stone stairway. On either side of a tunnel lined with limestone and mortar extend long narrow galleries for the placing of coffins. Some are private coffins and are fastened with wooden or iron doors, others are open. Some of the coffins can be seen lying in a scattered fashion, some have decayed throughout the years collapsing at the seams, giving a glimpse of an arm or leg sticking up. In one of these open chambers lies what is sought by every visitor, even though they will never say so, the four opened coffins. Here the coffin lids are off, exposing bodies partly covered with taut leathery skin, covered in a thick layer of dust.

Three of the coffins lie in a row across the front; a woman on the right, a man with a hand and both feet cut off in the centre – some say because he was a thief, others say so that the body could fit into the coffin. On the left is a nun. The coffin along the rear wall is that of the Crusader, the mummy believed to have been a soldier returned from the Crusades. His body has been cut in half, in order to fit in the coffin. One of his hands is lifted slightly in the air.

In another room you can see the coffins of the Sheare brothers who were executed by the British troops following the Rising of 1798. In 1998 their old coffins were replaced with new ones at the bicentennial commemoration. It was discovered that the standard British punishment for traitors was still in practice when these poor souls were executed for they had been hung, drawn and quartered.

In the church graveyard are other notables, including Oliver Bond, who took part in the 1798 Rising, and mathematician William Rowan Hamilton. It is generally thought that the remains of Robert Emmet, executed during the 1803 Rising, are also interred at St. Michan's.

The high concentration of lime is thought to account for the bodies being so well preserved, but it is no more so here than in other vaults around the city. Possibly it occurs because St. Michan's Church lies lower and nearer the bed of the Liffey.

The very dry atmosphere may be yet another reason the mummies have remained in a state of semi-preservation. Fascinating though it is, the Mummies of St. Michan's is not a tour for the faint-hearted. This is because strange whisperings and voices can be heard within the chambers.

Some visitors have reported being touched while bending down to look closely at the bodies. I became intrigued by the story and visited St. Michan's for myself. Strangely, I heard voices in the distance but brushed it off as the next group of tourists following along. This was until I said to one of the porters that the next group were a noisy bunch, to which he replied there was no group following and the next tour had not started!

St Michan's Church,
Church Street,
Dublin 8

The Brazen Head Pub

The Brazen Head pub dates back as far as 1198 and since then there has been a licensed premises on the location. How the pub acquired its name is of the great debate among its patrons. But the most likely explanation is linked to its location on the River Liffey. Up until 1670 the only bridge to cross the river was located at the Brazen Head. This was locally known as the head of the river. Soldiers who were on sentry lookout on the bridge on cold nights used to warm their hands on embers burning in barrels called "braziers" hence the name Braziers Head, eventually shortened to Brazen Head. The inn was located at what was then a crossroads of four major trading routes in Dublin making it a popular watering hole for Irish traders. The Brazen Head became a popular hotel boasting some forty-three rooms all located on the upper floors. Ireland's oldest piece of graffiti is also on the premises where on 7th August 1786 a Mr John Langan carved his name into one of the window panes with his diamond ring.

The Brazen Head Pub

As the Brazen Head matured through the centuries so did some of its famous patrons, many of whom were instrumental in the changing of Irish History. Some of the revolutionary figures that found safe haven within the walls were Michael Collins, Robert Emmet, Wolfe Tone, Oliver Bond and Daniel O'Connell. If you should visit the pub you will see their pictures hanging on the walls among the relics of Ireland's history. Robert Emmet was a regular guest in the hotel above the bar and always stayed in a room overlooking the laneway approaching the door to the inn, just to keep an eye on who was approaching. His writing desk is still in that very same room and it is alleged that the United Irishmen planned the 1798 rebellion within the walls of this famous inn. Robert Emmet was captured during the ill-fated 1803 uprising, tried, convicted and hanged on 20th September 1803 outside St. Catherine's Church on Cornmarket Street, less than 10 minutes walk from the Brazen Head pub. The Brazen Head is also famous for its Irish literary alumni such as Brendan Kennelly, Sean O'Casey, Brendan Behan and the famous James Joyce whose most famous literary work *Ulysses* featured the Brazen Head when Deadalus, one of Joyce's characters in the chapter Eumaeus, said "*you get a decent enough do in the Brazen Head.*" The spirit of Robert Emmet is reported to still wander the upper floors of the inn and staff have on several occasions become aware of being watched by some unseen entity that seems to be in the darker regions

Bar, The Brazen Head Pub

of the upper floors. Lights mysteriously switch themselves on and off unknown to staff who return wondering what's going on. Some staff have caught shadow-like movements out of the corner of their eyes. There is also a spirit that visits the older back rooms of the bar section where patrons of the pub have reported a sudden cold feeling coming over them as he passes by, probably heading to the bar for a refill of his favourite ale. Could this be Joyce, or another of the pub's famous past patrons?

The Brazen Head Pub is a pub where you will find some of Dublin's warmest people enjoying fine beer and music today much as they did back in 1198 when it first opened its doors to Dubliners. But do keep a wary eye open for you just might be drinking with some of the famous leaders of Irish history.

The Brazen Head Pub,
20 Lower Bridge Street,
Dublin

Phone: 01 6795186

The Ghost of 118 Summerhill

The following story appeared in the *Evening press* on 15th January 1966.

I'LL BUY THAT GHOST

Today demolition work was at a standstill in Summerhill's haunted house. No workmen turned up and the only person there apart from the ghost was in a striped apron, Mr Christopher McGregor one of the contractors.

From the doorway he surveyed the little groups of people who had gathered to have a look (from a safe distance) and said: "we have ten days to finish this job but it looks bad for today, and we got little work done yesterday on account of the crowds who wanted to see the ghost."

These crowds included an American who had read this paper's story and wanted a conducted tour. He got it.

Mr McGregor said "The fellow swore he saw a

shadow moving across that room up there. I followed his pointed finger and saw only the skeleton of a room without floor or ceiling. He then offered to buy the house on the spot. No sale was made.

That No. 118 summerhill is really haunted is no matter for doubt in the mind of any of the area's residents. In the grocer's shop at 35 Stoneybatter, Mr William Lynch told me the story of the ghost he knew of during the years he lived opposite the haunted house from 1904 to 1950.

He recounts: "There were three houses owned by the old wealthy Hutton family who were the last of the city's coach builders. I recall as a child seeing carriages drive up for big parties. But it was 117 which was haunted then. Crowds used to gather and wait for the ghosts to appear at midnight. I never saw it myself, but I do know that in those days there were people who would cross to the other side of the road passing 117. The ghost was supposed to have been seen at several different times at the window. The place had the look of a haunted house. It wasn't occupied, and the windows were barred and dust covered.

In 1923 the Hutton family sold out to the Dublin United Tramways Company, and the houses were converted into flats, then later deteriorating into tenements.

But the ghost stayed on. He moved into 118 when his haunt at 117 was pulled down.

Mr William McGregor, the senior contractor, saw the ghost and was shocked into a faint, and he wasn't the only man on the job who saw it.

The ghost will soon have to find a new home, or just

disappear, because 118 is the last of the old Hutton block. Local people would like it to settle down elsewhere.

This story sparked a series of replies to the Postbag section of the *Evening Press*.

On 18th January 1966 this story was published.

THE GHOST OF SUMMER HILL APPEARED
I remember a fatal fire at No. 118.

Are there any old residents of Summerhill or Parnell Street who remember the tragic history of the haunted house?

I was a young girl working in a shop in Parnell Street six years ago and I well remember the fire in 118 Summerhill in which five people were burned to death.

It was rumoured at the time that one of the tenants who had a flat there with his fourth wife had started the fire on purpose. Well his wife was killed as well as others. There was a big inquiry at the time, but nothing was proved, except the fire started on the stairs and trapped the victims. I also remember a white-haired, pale and hungry man who used to stand at the corner and I often give him a glass of milk and a bun and a few pence. He was the famous "skin the ghost" just out of prison. Eighty eight years young.

HE WAS WELL KNOWN

I was interested to read of the strange happenings at No 118 Summerhill. As a school boy in the 1920s the haunting of this house by a man was common knowledge to myself, sister and friends, even though we lived far from there. I wonder would it have appeared in any newspaper of the early or late twenties. Strange too none of the present neighbours have adverted to the fact. Perhaps most of the neighbours who knew left the district. *J.G.F, Dublin 3.*

But these letters also sparked a letter suggesting that the Ghosts did not exist at all.

This story appeared on Tuesday 25th 1966 in the *Evening Press.*

I NEVER HEARD OF THE GHOST!

I was very surprised to read about the ghost at 118 Summerhill. My father was born in that house 109 years ago and lived there until he married. My grandmother and aunt continued to live on at 118 until 1918. I have never heard of anyone living at 118 or the other two houses, 116 and 117, reporting the appearance of any ghost and there was no fire during their time. As a child living in Mountjoy Square I was in and out of the houses daily.

Miss Annette Hutton.

But one point we must remember about ghostly happenings is that although none of the residents living at the time experienced any happenings whatsoever, we cannot rule out the paranormal experience of residual energy. Residual energy is just a playback of an event or events in a building's past that has been stored up by the building. One major factor in residual energy being triggered is construction work or major changes to a building's structure. Now it has already been clearly established that No's 116 and 117 had already been knocked down. Could this construction work have been the trigger needed to start the residual energy, and could everyone be correct in as far as those who lived and played in 118 Summerhill did not experience anything paranormal. Did the builders see a ghost of a man wearing a striped apron like that of a butcher while they worked? The answer to this question we might never know but one thing is for certain it sparked a great deal of interest.

THE GHOST OF SUMMERHILL

I remember a fatal fire at No. 118

If there any old resident of Summerhill or Parnell Street who remembers the tragic history of the haunted house? I was a young girl working in a shop in Parnell Street 80 years ago and I well remember then too in 118 Summerhill in which four or five people were burnt to death.

It was rumoured at the time that one of the tenants who had set fire with his fourth wife had started the fire on purpose. We'll his wife was killed as well as others. There was a big inquiry at the time, but nothing was proved except the fire started on the stairs and trapped the victims. Maybe this was no such a blaze at once.

I also remember a whitehaired, pale and hungry man who used stand at the corner and often gave him a glass or milk and a loaf—and a few pence. He was the famous "Skin the Goat" just out of prison.

HE WAS WELL-KNOWN

I was interested to read of that strange happenings at No.

118 Summerhill. As a schoolboy in the 1930s the haunting of this house by a man was common knowledge to myself, sister and friends, even though we lived very far from there.

I wonder would it have appeared in any newspaper of the early or late twenties. Strange jim, some of the present neighbours have adverted to the fact. Perhaps most of the neighbours who knew not the disturbed.

Dublin, 2.

TELL US MORE, TERRY!

"Dubliner's Diary," ever interesting and entertaining, was never more so than on last Saturday night when Terry O'Sullivan asserted himself by opening his column with the startling and intriguing announcement that he "believed in ghosts and poltergeists."

Stating that some years ago he was convinced "against all belief" to apparently unbelievable and unreasonable events.

"Dubliner's Diary," ever intreating and entertaining, was never more so than on last which, he says, were capable of only being solved "by reason," in calmly makes us hanging to sudden in a state of frozen surprise by simply telling off with the almost Hitchcock-like anti-climactic statement that these facts have nothing to do with "Dubliner's Diary."

Could anything be more utterly tantalising? Instead of giving us even a glimmer or a glimmering of the gruesome events at which he hinted, he winds up merely re-stating the by that, well-known facts regarding the original ownership of No. 118 Summerhill by the famous Dublin coach building family of Hutton, whose daughter, Anne, married Thomas Davis, etc.

Naturally, one does not expect an up-to-date recording of the doings of the occult be a modern social columnist but, in this instance, Terry has said too much and too little to be allowed get away with it.

I am sure I am not alone in finding I can remember the first two or three paragraphs of "Dubliner's Diary" on Saturday, but, outside of the people concerned, who remembers that modern social columnist but, in this instance, Terry has said too much and too little to be allowed get away with it.

the supernatural, and I want to know more about it do love about H. Terry?

M. Keany, 32 St. Helen's Road, Booterstown, Dublin.

Tintern Abbey

Tintern Abbey at Bannow Bay, Co. Wexford was built by William Marshal, Earl of Pembroke in 1200. William set sail for Ireland on his first visit as Lord of Leinster, but was threatened with being shipwrecked by a raging storm in the Irish sea. He vowed to build an abbey wherever he could safely land, God willing.

William and his crew survived the storm and reached the safety of Bannow Bay. He redeemed his vow, bequeathing about 9,000 acres of land for a Cistercian abbey. Consequently Tintern Abbey was built on a site with a south-facing slope overlooking Tintern stream. Tintern Abbey is sometimes called Tintern de Voto "Tintern of the vow". Once established, the abbey was colonised by monks from the Cistercian abbey at Tintern in Monmouthshire, Wales, of which Marshal was also patron. In 1142 Marshal was part of sweeping reforms which took place in the Irish church in the 12th century.

The early Cistercians had their origins in the monastery of Citeaux in France. There they dedicated themselves to a simple life of prayer and manual labour.

By 1169, when the Anglo-Normans arrived in Ireland, there were already 15 Cistercian houses in Ireland. Following its foundation Tintern acquired large tracts of land in Co. Wexford and at the Dissolution of the Monasteries appears to have been the third richest Cistercian abbey in Ireland (after St. Mary's in Dublin). Constructed to the standard Cistercian plan, Tintern Abbey church was located to the north of an enclosed cloister which was surrounded on all sides by covered walks and a sequence of domestic buildings. Shortly after this Tintern Abbey and its lands were granted to Anthony Colclough from Staffordshire, an officer in Henry VIII's army.

The family home of Colclough which was established in Co. Wexford in the 16th century came to Ireland from Staffordshire in England. Anthony Colclough acquired Tintern Abbey in 1575. During the 17th and 18th centuries the Colcoughs were very prominent in that county and, compared with the earlier Anglo-Normans and faithful servants to the crown under Elizabeth 1, they were classed as "old English" and no less than fourteen Colcloughs suffered under the Williamite confiscation as "Irish Papists". Occasionally, however, one was found on the other side. Such was Capt. Thomas Coakley, who was rewarded in 1656 for his activity in "apprehending" Tories. Several of them held important offices in Counties Wexford and Kilkenny in the reign of James II and two at least were officers in his army. John Colclough, a Catholic landlord, was hanged on Wexford Bridge for his leading part in the Insurrection of 1798. Caesar Colclough (1766-1824), son of Sir Vesey Colclough of Tintern Abbey and M.P. for Wexford, was in France at the time of the French Revolution, which he supported. Another member of the Colclough family distinguished himself while serving with the Irish Brigade at Fontenoy. The family was still in possession of Tintern Abbey at the end of the last century when they possessed an estate of 13,000 acres in Co. Wexford.

The Colclough family extensively modified the abbey church, converting the crossing tower and later the nave, chancel and Lady Chapel to domestic quarters. In the 18th century Sir Vesey Colclough built many of the fine battlemented walls seen around the abbey today.

In the 1790s, John Colclough converted the nave into a residence of neo-Gothic style. He also established a flour mill, the ruins of which stand on the south bank of the stream close to the upper bridge. During this period also, a thriving weaving industry had developed in Tintern village, located across the stream south-west of the abbey. Following John's death, his brother Caesar inherited the estate and shortly after 1814 built the village of Saltmills to replace the old village of Tintern which was then demolished.

The final member of the Colclough family to reside at Tintern was Lucy Marie Biddulph Colclough who left in 1959, a few years before the abbey was taken into government care. Conservation and consolidation works started at Tintern in the early 1980s and archaeological excavations between 1982 and 1994 exposed many of the features of the original Cistercian abbey.

But today Tintern Abbey is reported to be haunted by the former monks of the abbey, for a ghostly phantom torch-lit procession of monks has been seen approaching the great entrance. This ghostly apparition has sometimes been accompanied by the sound of chanting monks. Locals have reported that late at night the ghostly procession makes its way into the great entrance where it disappears inside the walls of the abbey.

Tintern Abbey,
Bannow Bay,
Co. Wexford

Wicklow Gaol

Wicklow Gaol was built in 1702 and completed within a few years. The first recorded prisoner was a seventy-two year old priest Fr. Owen McFee who was convicted of saying Mass, contrary to the law at that time. Early conditions within the gaols at this time were appalling. Gaolers were paid a wage from the government, but many of the gaolers were themselves unsavoury characters. Sometimes inmates of the gaol with supervisory powers were corrupt and operated the gaol using bribery. For the poor prisoners who were imprisoned with no money or means to pay the gaoler life in the gaol was extremely harsh. It was only in 1763 that prison legislation enforced the separation of male and female prisoners. With the gaol's location to the port of Wicklow town it made for a prime deportation location for unsavoury prisoners that neither England nor Ireland wanted on its shores. Most of these prisoners where housed on the top level of the gaol in harsh conditions. Over 600 Irishmen who were involved in the 1798 Rebellion were deported. Of that number, approximately 105 were Wicklow men.

Because of the poor state of the gaol and the government's fear that it would not be able to support the large numbers housed within its walls due to the famine, Wicklow Gaol's status was demoted from that of a County Gaol to a Bridewell in 1877 by legislation. It was closed as

Wicklow Gaol

Floating orbs, Wicklow Gaol

a gaol in 1900 but soon re-opened in 1918 as a result of the Easter Rising. Manned by the Cheshire Regiment of the British Army, it housed members of the Irish Republican Brotherhood and Sinn Fein. Erskine Childers, one of Ireland's political leaders, was kept at the gaol prior to being brought to Dublin for execution following his capture at Glendalough House. The gaol closed again in 1924.

Today the gaol has been lovingly restored and makes for a great visit. Some of its inhabitants have chosen to remain behind and re-visit their one time place of incarceration. Staff and visitors to the gaol have on several occasions reported strange occurrences. On two separate

235

occasions young visitors have reported to the staff a kind and very helpful gentleman who they thought was part of the display because of his dress. Staff explained that there was no gentleman in the ship display, yet both described the exact same gentleman. In cell No. 5 on the ground floor, staff have often reported a strong sickening stench coming from within the cell. This became so bad on one occasion that it was sprayed with disinfectant. This cleared the smell but when staff returned there was no smell or odour even of the disinfectant, but a soothing smell of fresh flowers.

There are other spirits within the gaol which show themselves in the form of mists that move across the gantry from one side of the gaol to the other. There is even a mischievous spirit that will turn on the taps in the toilets just as the staff are entering them. As you walk around the gaol you cannot but only imagine the cramp hellish conditions that the prisoners suffered. Even whole families were kept with other prisoners in one cell. But, amazingly, considering its brutal past, there is not within the whole prison one malevolent or nasty spirit. It is a calm, peaceful place to visit and work. Today the gaol is open to the public as a national museum of early Irish prison life and is a worthwhile place to visit.

Wicklow Historic Gaol,
Kilmartin Hill,
Wicklow Town,
Co. Wicklow

Phone: 0404 61599

236

Wilton Castle

Looming above the landscape of South-eastern Ireland, only the fire-scarred walls remain of the once stately Wilton Castle. Harry Alcock of Wilton Castle was High Sheriff of Co. Wexford and Colonel of the Wexford Militia. Alcock was born on 22nd February 1792 and married Margaret Savage on 3rd September 1818. Margaret Savage, daughter and heir of James Savage of Kilgibon, was MP for Callan, in Co. Kilkenny. By his marriage Alcock inherited Kilgibon Estate, and they had four sons and five daughters. Harry Alcock died on 3rd December 1840, and was succeeded by his eldest son.

Colonel Alcock was industrious and spent much time and money carrying out improvements to the estate and restoring Wilton Castle. Colonel Alcock died without issue on 12th July 1893, and the property went to his nephew Philip Clayton Alcock, the last of the family to live in the parish.

Wilton Castle was destroyed by fire on 5th March 1923, as civil war raged throughout the country and burning out of landlords became a major pastime.

The Guardian newspaper report of the fire was carried on 10th March 1923. Here is the full account.

"Wilton Castle, the beautiful residence of Captain P.C. Alcock, which is situated about three miles from Enniscorthy was burned to the ground on Monday night last (5th March). The work of destruction was carried out by thirty men (this figure is questionable, by all accounts the number involved was much smaller), some of whom carried arms, and who as was subsequently ascertained, had also provided themselves with tins of petrol, with which they reduced Wilton to ashes, one of the best known residences in the Enniscorthy district. It was the fourth mansion in the Enniscorthy district to fall at the hands of the incendiaries (Bellevue, Coolbawn and Castleboro were the others), and in this respect the district should hold a record for the senseless work of destruction that is bound to serve no other purpose except to mulch the already over-burdened ratepayers in to providing the owners with compensation for the destruction of their beautiful homes.

Before the fire Wilton Castle was unoccupied for thirteen months. Its owner and his wife and family had to take up a temporary residence in Ludlow, Shropshire, their Irish home being left in the charge of a caretaker, Mr. James Stynes. Stynes occupied rooms in a portion of the castle. On a Monday night, shortly after 9pm the caretaker was visiting the steward's residence which was about 400 yards from the castle, when a loud knocking was heard on the door. The steward (Mr. George Windsor) answering the knock was confronted by a number of armed men who inquired for the caretaker, and when Mr. Stynes came forward he was requested to produce the keys of the castle. On enquiring the reason for the demand, the leader of the armed men said, "We have come to burn down the place, we are sorry."

Mr. Stynes tried to dissuade the men from their object, but failing, he asked for permission to remove the furniture from the building and also his own furniture. Permission was granted for him to remove his own belongings, but curt refusal was given regarding his employer's furniture. Having moved belongings, Mr. Stynes was ordered back to the steward's residence on which a guard was placed to prevent the alarm being raised.

When the caretaker and steward ventured out they were alarmed to see the beautiful building completely enveloped in flames. The raiders had done their work well. Every room was ablaze and with a wind blowing, flames were fanned and any attempt to save the building was hopeless. In a short time the roof caved in, floors collapsed and nothing remained of the once stately mansion but some begrimed roofless walls, broken windows and a smouldering heap of debris. Captain Alcock and his wife never again returned to Wilton and eventually the Irish Land Commission disposed of the lands to local people. Captain Alcock died on 6th January 1949 and was buried close to his Ludlow home at Overton Lodge. Mrs. Alcock died on 3rd July 1957. Captain Alcock had been suspicious of the caretaker long before the fire, and regretted afterwards that he had not entrusted a local person with the responsibility. Wilton is now a townland which rests peacefully holding the memories of many historic years, but generations of people are deprived of knowing the beauty and gracefulness of Wilton Castle in its true splendour.

Today a number of ghosts reside within the walls of the castle. One story tells of strange lights that are sometimes seen in the ruins of a castle tower where an old woman who was once an actress died in a fire. Then there is the tale that every year on the anniversary of his death the shadow of Harry Alcock, who died in 1840, is seen driving slowly away from the castle in a ghostly carriage. Crowds of locals once gathered in anticipation of the event. The strangest tale, however, is that of neighbour Archibald Jacob who served as a magistrate and captained the local militia company at the time of the rebellion against Britain in 1798. Jacob, who flogged and tortured many people in the parish, was returning home from a ball at Wilton Castle. Somehow his horse was startled and Jacob was killed by the fall from his horse. For years afterward his ghost was said to haunt both the scene of his death and the castle. On one occasion a Catholic priest was summoned to the castle to conduct an exorcism. It is wildly reported that when he made the sign of the cross the ghost of Archibald Jacob allegedly appeared in the fireplace then disappeared in a cloud of smoke.

Wilton Castle is located at Enniscorthy, Co. Wexford.

MUNSTER

Ballinacarriga Castle

The name Ballinacarriga in Irish is Beal na Carraige which
can mean either "the mouth" or "passage of rock".
Ballinacarriga Castle lies midway between Ballineen and
Dunmanway, overlooking Ballinacarriga Lough and along
the Bandon River. The Bandon River also supplied the
castle with fresh water in its days as a strong-hold. Today
the castle is a four storey tower built on a rocky eminence
with a good view in all directions. Ballinacarriga Castle is
unique for the stone carvings it contains mainly on what
was the third floor and is easily accessible by a circular
stone stairway built into the castle walls. These carvings
are religious in nature. In one of the window arches on the
top floor the Crucifixion shows Christ on the cross
between two thieves with the instruments of the passion;
a crown of thorns, a hammer and a heart pierced with two
swords. In the sofia on the north windows are the initials
"R.M. C.C." and the date 1585. These are believed to be

the initials of Randal Murlihy (Hurley) and his wife
Catherine Cullinane, and the date of the erection of the
building, although it is accepted that most of the castle is
older and may have been in the possession of the
MacCarthy family before Randal Hurley took possession.
The Hurley family reigned at the castle for over two
centuries. Catherine Cullinane's father was a famous doctor
from Bandon and Catherine and her family were colourful.
Their son Randal Óg allowed the local people to use the
castle as a church while their church was being built
nearby.

On the opposite windows are intricate carvings around
a chessboard design and there is also the figure of a
woman with five roses which is reported to be Catherine
Cullinane and her five children, whereas others say it's the
Virgin Mary. With the abundance of religious carvings on
this floor we can only assume that the top floor was used
as a chapel of the castle. The presence of a "Sheila na Gig"
above and to the right of the main door of the castle would
appear to substantiate this, as these unusual female figures
are often found on the outside walls of medieval churches.

Outside to the southeast is the remnant of one of the
castle's four defence towers, which guarded the main
tower of the castle against attack.

On the second floor there is a mural gallery (that is
built into the walls) leading to the garderobe, or lavatory,
which is on the north side over a chute. For some reason
this is known as "Moll the Phooka's Hole". The Pooka, or
phooka, is a type of Irish hobgoblin who can appear in
many different shapes and forms. Usually he has red eyes

and some sort of fire-breathing properties. He mostly appears in the shape of a dark coloured large animal resembling a horse, a pony or even a very large goat. Sometimes he appears as a giant bull with eyes and nostrils gleaming fire. He has often been described as a very large eagle-like creature. The time of year usually associated with the pooka is *Samhain* or Halloween, the last day of October. This is the time when the Celts believed the barriers between our material world and the otherworld to be at their weakest. The Pooka usually crept up silently behind his victim and if he succeeded in getting his head between the victim's legs they were whisked up on his back, then he could take them anywhere – to the highest peak or the lowest depth or to any place on the face of the earth.

The castle is reported to have been occupied by a garrison of Cromwell's men for a time and when they were leaving they would have removed the overhanging parapets, thus depriving the castle of its main defence against further attack. But it is the Phooka that still haunts Ballinacarriga Castle. These evil creatures drove fear into the Irish peasants. The Phookas were reported to be able to fly short distances and were freed for taking young babies, causing crops to fail and inflicting immense harm on the local people. But it was the foul smelling garderobe or lavatory that was reported to be the most suitable access to the castle for these smelly creatures.

Ballinacarriga Castle is located off the main road from Ballineen to Dunmanway in Co. Cork.

Bantry House

The original house was built by Samuel Hutchinson around 1720 and was a five-bay three-storey building called Blackrock. It formed the nucleus of the present Bantry House. In 1746 it was acquired by Richard White, a farmer from Whiddy Island who had amassed a fortune from pilchard fishing, iron smelting and probably from some smuggling. Richard White also acquired most of the land around Bantry including large parts of the Beare Peninsula, estates which were further enlarged by his grandson Richard White (1767-1851). The young Richard took little interest in social or political affairs, preferring to live quietly at Bantry. But in December 1796 a formidable French Armada, inspired by Theobald Wolfe Tone and the United Irishmen and under the command of Admiral Hoche, sailed from Brest in France. Young Richard was unexpectedly thrust into the limelight when a French fleet sailed into Bantry Bay to join forces with the United

Irishmen. Their purpose was to invade Ireland and put an end to British rule, also to establish an independent Irish republic. Almost 50 warships carrying 15,000 soldiers set sail for the South-west of Co. Cork.

Richard White, the owner of Bantry House, alerted by rumours of the possible invasion had already raised a militia, most of them his own tenants who were loyal to himself and the British crown. He armed and trained them, and their muskets and power kegs were stored in the basement of Bantry House for safe keeping. By mid-December that year he had posted look-outs at the furthest seaward reaches of his land (Mizen Head, Sheeps Head) and riders on good horses to bring news as soon as the French fleet was sighted.

Richard had luck on his side, for a huge storm interrupted ship-to-ship communication and the invasion foundered, causing the fleet to eventually turn for home.

Ten of the fifty ships did not return. One of these, the *Surveillante* was too storm damaged to make the return passage to France and she was scuttled off Whiddy Island, opposite Bantry House.

For his part in this matter, Richard White was made Baron Bantry in 1797 and in 1816 he was created Earl of Bantry.

The *Surveillante* lay undisturbed for almost 200 years, was rediscovered in 1982, and declared an Irish National Monument in 1985 when work began on her recovery and conservation.

The Armada Centre records this amazing episode of Irish history and includes an individual sound tour, complete with accompanying music and sound effects, in a choice of several languages.

The centrepiece of the exhibition is a large one-to-six scale model of the frigate *Surveillante* in cross section, showing details of her construction and typical activities that took place on board.

Although some modifications to the house appear to have occurred during the 1770s, most of the additions and alterations took place during the first Earl's lifetime. A two-storey addition with bowed ends and a six-bay front facing onto Bantry Bay were added in 1820, providing additional space for two large drawing-rooms and several

Bantry House

bedrooms above. Many more substantial changes were
made in 1845 by Richard, Viscount Berehaven (1800-67),
a passionate art collector who travelled regularly across
Europe visiting Russia, Poland, France and Italy and
bringing back shiploads of exotic goods between 1820 and
1840. To accommodate his new furnishings the Viscount
built a fourteen bay block to the rear of the old house
consisting of a six-bay centre of two storeys over a
basement flanked by four-storey bow-ended wings.

After his death in 1867 the property was inherited by
his brother William, the third Earl (1801-84). William
married Jane Herbert in 1846, the daughter of John
Herbert of Muckross. They had four daughters: Elizabeth,
Olive, Ina and Jane who sadly died while still an infant.
They also had one son William. From 1860 to 1870 Bantry
House saw happy times with many a ball being held at the
house. In 1884 William died and was succeeded by his son
William and in 1886 the new Earl married Rosamond
Petre, daughter of the Honourable George Petre. Sadly
William did not enjoy the long life of his father and died
in 1891 with no heirs to his name so his titles became
extinct.

Bantry House remained with the family and passed to
William's nephew Edward, son of William's eldest sister
Elizabeth who had married Egerton Leigh of Cheshire.
Edward was born in 1876 and assumed the name White in
1897. In 1904 he married Arethusa Hawker of Longparish
Hampshire. They had two daughters, Clodagh and
Rachel. Edward Leigh-White died in 1920 leaving Bantry
House to his eldest daughter Clodagh then a girl of just 15

years old. Also in 1920 the local hospital run by nuns burned down and Bantry House offered its services as a makeshift hospital. In 1926 Clodagh became of age and took responsibility for the estate. Also in this year she met Geoffrey Shelswell of Essex. Geoffrey was a member of the British colonial services. Clodagh and Geoffrey married and had three children: Delia, Oonagh and Egerton.

In 1945 Clodagh took the decision that insured the future of Bantry House. She opened it up to the public, the first in Ireland to be displayed. Geoffrey died in 1962, leaving Clodagh to run and show Bantry House to the public. Then in March 1978 after a short and painless illness Clogagh died and left Bantry House to her only son Egerton Shelswell-White.

Today, Bantry House remains much as the second Earl left it with an important part of his great collection still intact.

It is up in the nursery area of Bantry House that the present lady of the house Brigitte Shelswell-White felt a presence around her. For one day Brigitte was working in that area when she felt someone come up close to her from behind. Brigitte initially thought it was one of the workers from the house, standing a little two close for comfort, as if they were invading her private space. She turned to see who this was, but there was nobody in the room, not even up in that part of the house. Brigitte described the feeling to me as a strange yet comforting feeling, not threatening or malevolent, as if someone who knew her was letting her know that it was alright. There was a butler that died within the walls of the house. Could this be his spirit still caring for the owners? Or is it a long-deceased relative popping back to see their loved ones? We will never know until they are ready to let us know who they are.

Bantry House is a magical and romantic house to visit, from the moment you step through the door you step back in time. I was not sure whether it was because the house has not changed through time, or if there was a strong presence of residual energy within the house, because every room I entered or corner I turned I could feel as if the house was alive.

Bantry House,
Bantry,
Co. Cork

Carrigaholt Castle

Carrigaholt Castle, Co. Clare is set on the verge of a cliff overlooking the Shannon Estuary. This tall, well-preserved tower house built around the end of the 15th century by the Teige (Caech) MacMahon, chief of the Corcabascin, has five storeys with a vault on the fourth floor and most of the usual tower-house features, such as a murder hole inside the entrance, a mural winding stair and pistol loops.

The castle was occupied by Teige Caech, "the short-sighted" MacMahon, in September 1588 when seven ships of the Spanish Armada anchored at Carrigaholt. Although aid was refused by the MacMahons, the castle was none the less unsuccessfully besieged shortly afterwards by Sir Conyers Clifford. The following year the renegade fourth Earl of Thomond captured it after a four-day siege and, in breach of the surrender terms, hanged all the defenders. Ownership then passed to the Earl's brother Donal, who was responsible for inserting many of the castle's windows as well as the fireplace on the fifth floor, which bears the date 1603. Donal's grandson was the celebrated third

Viscount Clare who resided at Carrigaholt and raised a regiment of horses known as the "Yellow Dragoons" for James II's armies. After the forfeiture of his extensive 57,000 acre estate by the Williamites, the castle was acquired by the Burton family who held it until the present century.

In 1646 Admiral Sir William Penn called at the castle on his way to Kinsale, having just abandoned Bunratty to the Confederate troops. In 1651 it was taken by Cromwell's general, Ludlow, who kept a garrison there

Carrigaholt Castle

Carrigaholt Castle

until 1652. Charles 11, however, restored the castle to the O'Briens in 1666. But in 1691 William of Orange gave it to Keppel, Earl of Albermarle, who sold it almost immediately afterwards to the Burtons who retained it up until the present century. The bawn protecting the tower is fairly well preserved, though the turret overlooking the pier is modern. Legend has it that in McMahon's Castle in Co. Clare there is a sealed room in the derelict shell containing an evil so great that no one has looked upon it and lived to tell the tale. The last time that the stones which seal this chamber were opened was in the late 1920s. The exorcist then descended into this chamber to deal with whatever dreadful creature was lurking within.

He was found the next morning, lying in the remains of what would have been the great hall. His death certificate recorded cause of death as heart failure. But apparently no one who saw the poor man could ever forget the look of terror engraved into his cold face.

Carrigaholt Castle is located 7 miles South West of Kilkee on the West side of the jetty at Carrigaholt. Co. Clare.

Charles Fort Castle

Charles Fort Castle was constructed during the late 17th century on the site of an earlier coastal fortification and with five bastions is a classic example of a star-shaped fort. The two seaward bastions known as the Devil's and the Charles were for defending the harbour and had gun embrasures inside as well as on top of the walls.

The North, Flagstaff and the Cockpit are the three landward bastions and all three had a brick sentry box at their outermost point, two of which survive today.

The site of Charles Fort castle belonged to the Barry Oges family until 1601 when it was occupied by a Spanish force and subsequently stormed by Mountjoy's troops. In 1668 the site was chosen by the Earl of Orrey for an earthwork fort built with outer and inner lines of ramparts allowing for two tiers of guns overlooking the sea.

The construction of the present Charles Fort began in 1677, and was designed by Sir William Robinson, the

Surveyor General, in co-operation with James Archer who oversaw the work. The castle crumbled in October 1690 when it was besieged by the Williamite general, the Duke of Marlborough who succeeded by placing his cannon on the high ground and breaching the wall of the castle. After a siege that lasted twelve days, Sir Edward Scott and 1,000 of his men surrendered on honourable terms and marched out through the breach in the walls followed by Lady Scott in her carriage.

In 1694 the fort was rebuilt by the Huguenot military engineer Rudolph Corneille, following the original plans. A barracks for over 300 men was added in the 19th century. In 1922 the army handed over the fort to the Irish Irregulars who subsequently burnt it down. In 1973 the Irish castle was declared a National Monument and renovated. Charles Fort castle is reported to be haunted by the spirit of a young girl who died on her wedding night. The story is as follows:

On their wedding night the happy couple walked arm in arm along the ramparts of the castle. As they reached the land-side part of the castle the young bride suddenly stopped, having spotted a solitary white rose down along the battlements. She pointed the rose out to her new husband. A sentry overheard the girl expressing a wish for the rose and immediately volunteered to climb down and get it for her. Not wanting to get into trouble the sentry asked her husband to stand guard while he retrieved the rose. The bridegroom agreed to this and took the sentry's musket. The sentry then clambered over the wall and disappeared. Standing in the sentry post the young husband awaited the man's return with his bride beside him. Time passed and there was no sign of the sentry. Assuming the man had met with some unforeseen delay in securing the rose the bridegroom sent the bride indoors while he waited a while longer at the sentry-post. After a while in the peaceful surroundings of the sentry post he dozed off. The girl's father and Commander of the Fort was out on his inspection of the castle and came upon what he thought was one of his sentries asleep while on duty. At the time it was customary in military service to be executed if found asleep while on duty. Without realizing that the nodding man was not the sentry but his son-in-law he drew his pistol and shot the sleeping man. Then tormented by what he had just done and in a fit of guilt the commander threw himself off the ramparts. The bride returned to her husband thinking he had recovered the rose for her but found him dead. Looking over the ramparts she saw the body of her father on the rocks beneath the walls. The grief-stricken bride could take no more and jumped over the ramparts to her death below.

This gave birth to the ghost of the "White Lady". She has on several occasions been seen walking the ramparts of the castle, a beautiful young woman with a beautiful white face and a long flowing white dress.

Charles Fort Castle,
Kinsale,
Co. Cork
Phone: 021 4255100

McCarthy's Pub, Fethard

Established by Richard McCarthy in the 1850s McCarthy's provided quite a few services for the town of Fethard. Among these were a spirit merchant, restaurant, hotel, undertaker, draper, grocer, baker, hackney service, glass, delph and china shop, and if you still couldn't get what you wanted McCarthy would hire a few horses to take you elsewhere to get it. Today the McCarthys still run a pub, restaurant and undertaker business from the very same location they first traded from in 1850. McCarthy's success is based on a mix of the old and the new. The interior is unchanged since Richard McCarthy opened for business in the 1850s. McCarthys were lucky that in the 1970s, when great changes swept Ireland, three old ladies, Beatty, Kitty and Nell, ruled the pub and were unwilling to modernise the premises to a "lounge bar". People still return expecting to meet the old ladies (now sadly deceased and missed by the community of Fethard) sitting in the office, drinking tea and surveying the comings and goings of life from the office door. Thoughout the years the McCarthys were closely involved with sport and had a particular interest in horses. Dick McCarthy was a professional jockey who also played hurling, football, rugby, polo and was a champion amateur Irish boxer. His brothers Gus and Chris McCarthy were also amateur jockeys. Gus was also a noted footballer who won an all-Ireland medal with Tipperary and also played on the ill-fated Bloody Sunday Tipperary team in Croke Park on 21st November 1920. The current generation are as keenly involved in both horses and Gaelic games.

McCarthy's Pub, Fethard

McCarthy's also has a rich paranormal history. A sign was given before the deaths of the last generation of McCarthys. This was usually in the form of a picture falling from the wall for no apparent reason. Other incidents of near death warnings were three loud knocks on the front door. These knocks were heard by people at both sides of the door before Beattie's death. Ghosts were spotted recently by Mark Lonergan and John O'Connor at night and by Ciarán Hayes in the afternoon within the pub. These strange happenings have continued up to the present day. In February 2006 the picture fell off the wall again and another member of the family passed away. I often wondered if all these strange occurrences that are happening in McCarthy's pub have anything to do with the fact that they also ran an undertakers, that just happens to be next door to the pub. Could the spirits of the deceased that are lying in the undertakers pop next door to the pub and join in their own wake? Or are past members of the McCarthy family still keeping an eye on the family business?

So next time you see somebody sitting quietly sipping a pint in the corner – you might be the only one who can see him!

McCarthy's Pub,
Main Street,
Fethard,
Co. Tipperary

Phone 052 31194

Monasteranenagh
Cistercian Abbey

Monasteranenagh Cistercian Abbey derives its name from Manister an Aonaigh, the monastery of the fair, after a fair that was held on the site in ancient times. Today the ruins consist of a church that dates from 1170 and an early Gothic chapter house. It is reported that locals buried stillborn children within the ruins of the Abbey's chapter house. Located in a valley about two miles east of the village of Shanagolden, Co. Limerick it is one of the earliest recorded nunneries in Ireland.

The ruins are quite extensive, and are in good condition. Sadly the tower fell in 1806 and the roof collapsed in 1874. Only walls and gables remain of the church. The interior of the abbey was used as a burial ground until the 1970s. In 1228 the abbey saw its first conflict when the Irish monks with the help of the O'Brien's, the Kings of Thomond, drove out the abbot and the non-Irish monks who were of Norman descent. They were excommunicated for "revolting against their ecclesiastical superiors". Using armed force, Hubert de Burgo the bishop of Limerick, recaptured the abbey, and reinstalled the monks who had been driven out.

In 1540 the monastery at Manister was dissolved, although the monks were left in possession of the abbey.

In 1579 the abbey saw its second and final conflict when Sir William Malby led the English in a battle against the Irish and Spaniards. Sir John of Desmond led the Irish. The Earl of Desmond saw the battle from Tory Hill. The English fired at Irish and Spanish soldiers who were sheltered in the abbey causing great damage to the building.

However, the monastery was not destroyed until 1585, when it became the property of Sir Henry Wallop. Sir Henry plundered and robbed all of its valuables before destroying the monastery.

Prior to the dissolution in 1540 it was said that the last abbess practiced witchcraft in a room to the south of the church which is now known as the "The Black Hag's Cell". It is possible that this legend was probably propaganda in furtherance of the Dissolution of the Monasteries.

The second legend is connected to the Earl of Desmond. Whilst the Earl and Countess of Desmond were escaping the nunnery the Countess was wounded by an arrow. So serious was the attack, that the Earl believed his wife to have died from the wound and had her buried beneath the altar in the main chapel. However, she subsequently awoke to find herself buried alive and her screams are said to echo through the ruins to this day.

Monasteranenagh Cistercian Abbey,
Shanagolden, Co. Limerick

ULSTER

Bonamargy Friary

Bonamargy Friary is one of the finest ruins along the north coast. It was originally a thatched friary. Today the ruins consist of a chapel, vaults, gatehouse, cloisters, living quarters and a graveyard. The name Bun na Mairge means the foot of the Margy (the combined Glenshesk and Carey rivers) and the friary is sited where these rivers approach the sea. Rivers and sea were both important to the friars for food and transport. Some archives date this Third Order Franciscan Friary to around 1500, others put it around the 1480s.

The Franciscans first arrived in Ireland in 1226 and for the first hundred years they remained relatively small due to politics, war and the Black Death. By the early 1430s the third Order was founded in Ireland. The MacQuillen family founded Bonamargy friary and they can be traced to the Norman de Mandevilles, but it later came into the possession of the MacDonnells when Sorley Boy

MacDonnell defeated the MacQuillen in a battle 1558, and effectively became "Lord of the Route". In 1584 the church was burned (its thatched roof is mentioned) when Irish and Scots attacked English troops quartered there, but was repaired. Even after the friars of the Third Order withdrew in the early 17th century the buildings were used by other Franciscans, partly as a base for missionary work in Scotland. The friary was probably abandoned by the end of the 17th century, but continued to be used for burial.

Several of the Earls of Ulster are interred in the Friary, including Sorley Boy MacDonnell. It also became the focal point during the first half of the 15th century for missionary work to Scotland. It is widely reported that by the 1600s there were only twelve priests left in Scotland and the religion was in danger of extinction, whereas in the north and west of Ireland the Reformation by King Henry had a dramatic effect on Catholicism throughout Scotland.

Bonamargy Friary was granted to members of the First Order of Franciscans in 1626 as a rest house for those doing missionary work in the Highlands and Isles. During the late 1630s Bonamargy became a refuge for Scots men and women returning to the Catholic faith. In 1639 there are accounts of the Franciscan Bishop of Down and Connor Bonaventure Magennis confirming nearly 700 people from Scotland in Bonamargy and in 1640 Father Hegarty, Guardian of the Friary, informed the Vatican that over 1000 people had been reconciled with the Church at Bonamargy.

The friary was in use up until the early 18th century when the last friars left in 1790. After this time local stories tell of a Julie MacQuillen living in the monastery. She was known as the black nun of Bun na Mairge and is believed to have prophesised many events, some of which came true. Others are still outstanding, but even here there is some dispute about what exactly were her thoughts on the future. The seven prophesised events were:

(1) Boats would be made of iron. (2) Knocklayde would burst and the water pouring from it would flood land for seven miles around. One other version of this says a man would be able to press a button and water would flow from Knocklayde to Ballycastle. (3) A red-haired lady would fall off Fairhead. (4) Ireland would become independent with the arrival of a sailing ship with her sails on fire. (5) Horseless carriages. (6) The Milltown river would flow with blood.

Legend today tells the story of Julie MacQuillen's murder on the stone stairs leading up to the second floor of the friary, and she still haunts these steps at night. A small cross with a hole through the centre near the west gable of the chapel is believed to mark her grave. Another story tells of the friars, before fleeing from the friary during one of the many raids, having buried the friary's valuables at the furthest reach of the light from a candle burning in the east window of the chapel. The friary is steeped in a wealth of history from being attacked and burnt to it being used as a billet and stables for soldiers. To the left of the main Friary is a small lodge house. In 1822 a small oak chest was found in the chimney which

271

contained manuscripts in illuminated Latin script believed to have been written in the 12th century and part of the theological work of St. Thomas Aquinas (1224 -1274). St. Thomas belonged to the monastery of St. Anthony of Delestmon. St.Thomas Aquinas was of the Dominican Order and travelled widely during his life, he was considered one of the greatest Christian philosophers to have lived. Two of his most famous works were the "Summa Theologiae" and the "Summa Contra Gentiles". He was prolific in the amount of work he produced during his lifetime and it is known that he was a close friend of a Franciscan monk called Bonaventure who later in 1237 became the minister general of the Franciscan Order. They studied together in Paris and received their Doctorates in Theology at the same time. Though how his work, if indeed it was his work, arrived in Bonamargy Friary is still a mystery. Also in Bonamargy you will find the graves of seamen from HMS Racoon and HMS Viknor. HMS Racoon was lost at the Garvin Isles, Donegal and HMS Viknor struck a mine and sank off Tory Island. Both had no survivors.

The present physical condition of Bonamargy Friary owes much to conservation by the Belfast Natural History and Philosophical Society in 1931. It was placed in State care by Ballycastle Rural District Council in 1933.

Bonamargy Friary,
Bonamargy,
Co. Antrim,
North of Ireland

272

Carrickfergus Castle

Once the centre of Anglo-Norman power in Ulster, the mighty stronghold of Carrickfergus is a remarkably complete and well-preserved early medieval castle that has survived intact despite 750 years of continuous military occupation. Originally almost surrounded by sea, the castle commanded Belfast Lough.

The core of the castle was built by John de Courcy, who conquered east Ulster in 1177 and ruled as a petty king until 1204, when he was ousted by another Norman adventurer Hugh de Lacy. The inner ward was initially built by de Courcy

Following its capture in 1210 by King John, Carrickfergus Castle passed to the Crown and constables were appointed to command the castle. In 1217 the new constable appointed De Serlane, who was assigned £100 to build a new curtain wall to protect the approach along the rocks as well as the eastern approaches over the sandy

exposed area at low tide. In the 18th century the middle-
ward curtain wall was then later reduced to ground level,
apart from along the seaward side where it survives with
a postern gate and the east tower.

After being restored to the Ulster Earldom in 1227,
Hugh de Lacy returned to Carrickfergus, where he
remained until his death in 1242. It was almost certainly
de Lacy who enclosed the remainder of the promontory to
form an outer ward, doubling the area of the castle. Both
towers were originally circular in plan but during the 16th
century were cut in half and lowered in height to
accommodate artillery.

It is believed that the chamber on the first floor of the
east tower was the castle's chapel on account of its fine
Romanesque-style double window surround. The original
chapel of the first building must have been in the inner
ward. The ribbed vault over the entrance passage, the
murder hole and the massive portcullis at either end of the
gatehouse are later additions, probably part of the
rebuilding that followed Edward Bruce's long and bitter
siege of 1315-1316.

After the collapse of the Earldom of Ulster in 1333, the
castle remained the Crown's principal residential and
administrative centre in the North of Ireland. During the
16th and 17th centuries a number of improvements were
made to accommodate artillery, notably externally splayed
gun-ports and embrasures for cannons, though these
improvements did not prevent the castle from being
attacked and captured on many occasions during this time.
When General Schomberg besieged and took the castle in

1690, its importance was already in decline. In 1760 it was captured and held by French invaders under the command of Thurot. Later it served as a prison and during the Napoleonic Wars was heavily defended; six guns on the east battery remain of the twenty-two that were used in 1811. For a century it remained a magazine and armoury before being transferred to the government in 1928 for preservation as an ancient monument.

Carrickfergus Castle has another historical side. Robert Rainey was a soldier who was stationed at Carrickfergus Castle around the 1760s. Let's say he was a man with a reputation for the ladies. He was to fall in love with a local girl named Betsy Bird and made a vow never again to stray and to be faithful should she marry him. She considered his proposal and Robert was overjoyed, but unknown to Robert Betsy was also seeing the brother of Robert's commanding officer Colonel Jennings. How Robert discovered that his fiancee was being unfaithful is still unknown, but what is known is Robert's reaction to the news. He made off in search of his adversary and found him on the road outside the castle. Calmly Robert drew his sword and ran it through his fiancee's lover and calmly sheeted his sword and returned to his quarters where he washed away any incriminating blood stains from his clothing and weapon. Fortunately or unfortunately for Robert, Jennings did not die straight away. He was discovered by his brother and gave the name of Timothy Lavery as his attacker. Lavery was also stationed at the castle and had an uncanny likeness for Robert. The poor unfortunate Lavery, despite his plea of innocence, was charged with murder and on the day of his execution, as the noose was placed around his neck, he vowed to return and haunt the castle of Carrickfergus. Robert Rainey confessed to his wrongdoing some years later, but that was too late for Lavery. Timothy Lavery's spirit still haunts the castle of Carrickfergus and his demented spirit has been seen around the deep dark well hole in the castle.

Carrickfergus Castle,
Marine Highway,
Carrickfergus,
Co. Antrim

Castle Leslie

The Leslie family can trace their ancestry back as far as
Atilla The Hun. The first member of the Leslie family
came from Scotland. Bartholomew Leslie was a Hungarian
nobleman and Chamberlain and Protector of Margaret
Queen of Scots. While fleeing enemies, Queen Margaret
rode pillion on the back of Bartholomew's horse, but while
crossing a river the queen fell off.

Bartholomew threw her the end of his belt and told her
to grip fast the buckle. It is because of this heroic act that
the Queen bestowed the motto "Grip Fast" on the Leslie
family. A majestic tapestry baring the family coat of arms
with the motto still hangs in the castle today. The first
Leslie to come to Ireland was bishop John Leslie, bishop
of the isle of Scotland. He was known as the "fighting
Bishop" and defeated Cromwell's army at the Battle of
Raphoe. With the restoration of Charles II, the bishop,
who was then ninety rode from Chester to London in

twenty four hours. For his loyalty the king granted him a reward of £2000. In 1665 Glaslough castle was sold by Sir Thomas Ridgeway to John Leslie. The bishop enjoyed the castle till his death at the age of 100 in 1671.

Castle Leslie

This began the long legacy of the Leslie family in Ireland and Irish history. Charles Powell Leslie took over the estate in 1743. Charles devoted himself to the improvement of farming methods in the district. He was elected M.P. for Hillsborough in 1771 and M.P. for Monaghan in 1776. But it was in 1779 that he became very active in the great Volunteer movement and became Colonel of the Trough Volunteers. In 1783 Grattan's Parliament was established from 80,000 Volunteers. Charles represented the County Of Monaghan and in his election speech of 1783 stated 'I desire a more equal representation of the people and a tax upon our Absentee Landlords'.

They say that the Battle of Waterloo was won on the playing fields of Eton. But some historians think it was won at Castle Leslie, when Charles Powell Leslie decided to help his impoverished brother-in-law, Lord Mornington, professor of Music at TCD, to educate his son Arthur. Had he not done so Arthur would never have grown up to become Duke of Wellington and defeat Napoleon at Waterloo. But for me the most famous member of the Lesley family is Norman Leslie son of Sir John Leslie, lst Bt, 1848-1891 and Lady Constance 1835-1925. Norman followed in his father's steps and joined the military. A typical gentleman of his time, he even engaged in a duel with a Yusoury Pasha in Paris in 1910, after being discovered in an assignation in Cairo with Yusoury's wife. Duelling was forbidden in the British army, but not to do so would have meant losing respect among the Egyptians. The then Duke of Connaught intervened. A committee consisting of Lord Cromer, Lord Charles Beresford and Sir Ernest Cassel advised Norman that it would be safe to proceed with the duel if it was kept from the newspapers. Norman underwent fencing tuition with a French fencing master. The duel was fought in Paris, and technically Norman drew first blood in the duel but they continued to duel for 40 minutes, eventually ending when Norman received a hand wound. He returned to Cairo to convalesce, having given an undertaking not to communicate with the lady, except through her husband. But it was while fighting in the first world war that Norman Leslie met his death.

He was killed near Armentières, France on 18th October 1914 while charging a German machine gun. But on that same fateful day on the doorsteps of Castle Leslie the staff of the castle saw what they knew to be Norman Leslie walk into the castle dressed in his military uniform. The

Castle Leslie graveyard

rumour that Norman had returned spread through the castle until Lady Constance came to hear of it. She instinctively knew that her son was dead and began to prepare his room for the arrival of his body. Her feelings were proved correct when two days later she received a telegram from the British Army informing her that her son had been killed in action in Armentières while fighting the German army. Since then some visitors to the castle have reported to the staff that while sleeping in Norman's room they may have felt the presence of a spirit. Other guests have reported seeing ghostly spirits walking the corridors of the castle as if carrying out their daily duties. Does Norman still visit the castle today? I'd like to think he does, as with all the spirits of the Leslie family.

A stay in Castle Leslie is a must for any paranormal investigator.

Castle Leslie,
Glaslough,
Co. Monaghan

Phone: 047 88109
Or e-mail info@castleleslie.com

Dobbins Inn

Around 1200AD Reginald D'Aubin was granted a piece of land beside the newly completed Carrickfergus Castle. Seventeen of the D'Aubins were sheriffs and eight were mayors of Carrickfergus between 1571 and 1666.

Reginald set about building a tower house for himself and his family which remained in the possession of his descendents for hundreds of years. By the 15th century the family name of D'Aubin had been changed to Dobyn and successive generations became important local dignitaries, several holding high civic office. In the reign of King James I, during the Plantation of Ulster, their house became a shelter for Catholic priests who would celebrate secret masses on the premises, and a priest's hole dating from those troubled times is still visible in the hotel's reception. During the deadly feuds which existed in the Middle Ages, when no man was secure from spies and traitors even within the walls of his own house, it is no matter of wonder that the castles and mansions of the powerful and wealthy were usually provided with some precaution in the event of a sudden surprise. A secret means of concealment or escape was required so that it could be used at a moment's notice. A majority of these secret chambers and hiding-places in our ancient buildings owe their origin to religious persecution, particularly during the reign of Elizabeth, when the most stringent laws and oppressive burdens were inflicted upon all persons who professed the tenets of the Church of Rome.

In the first years of the virgin Queen's reign all who clung to the older forms of the Catholic faith were mercifully frowned upon, as long as they solemnised their own religious rites within their private dwelling-houses. After the Roman Catholic rising in the north and numerous other Popish plots, the utmost severity of the law was enforced, particularly against seminaries. The chief object was, as was generally believed, to stir up their disciples in England against the Protestant Queen. An Act was passed prohibiting a member of the Church of Rome from celebrating the rites of his/her religion on pain of forfeiture for the first offence. A year's imprisonment for the second, and imprisonment for life for the third. All those who refused to take the Oath of Supremacy were called "recusants" and were guilty of high treason. A law was also enacted which provided that if any Papist should convert a Protestant to the Church of Rome, both should suffer death, as for high treason.

It was during this period that the inn acquired its resident ghost, for it was not only priests who used these

(Footnote 1: In December, 1591, a priest was hanged before the door of a house in Gray's Inn Fields for having there said Mass the month previously.)

secret hidings and escape places. When Elizabeth Dobbins, wife of the owner Hugh Dobbins, fell in love with a handsome soldier stationed at the castle opposite, she would creep through this secret tunnel at night in order to enjoy a romantic liaison with her soldier love, remembered simply as "Buttoncap". The entrance to the tunnel is still evident at the back of the stone fireplace in the hotel's reception.

But when her husband discovered their affair he was so furious at her betrayal that he put both of them to death with his sword. Elizabeth's ghost is reported to have wandered the inn ever since.

In 1946 the old property was converted into a hotel and the spirit of Elizabeth – or Maude, as she for some reason became known – lingered on as its oldest resident. Several guests have been wakened from their sleep by the lightest touch of a ghostly unseen hand caressing their faces. Others have caught glimpses of a furtive figure flitting across reception and disappearing close to the stone fireplace. Could this be the spirit of Elizabeth still sneaking out for a secret liaison with her secret lover? Dobbins Inn was recently investigated by a local paranormal investigation group. They brought along a medium who claimed to have picked up on the presence of eight spirits in total within the inn.

Dobbins Inn,
6-8 High Street,
Carrickfergus, Co. Antrim

Phone: 048 9335 1905
email: info@dobbinsinnhotel.co.uk

Dunluce Castle

This 17th century medieval castle is one of the most dramatically sited of all of the Irish castles. Perched on a headland dropping sheer into the north Atlantic sea on the north Antrim Coast, the first castle to be documented on this site was built by the McQuillan family in 1513 and later became the stronghold of the McDonnells in the 16th century. The McDonnells were the Earls of Antrim and Lords of the Isles. During the McDonnell ownership of Dunluce Castle it was taken by Somhairle Buidhe, Sorley Boy MacDonnell (1508-1589), whose brother had married the daughter of McQuillan. In 1556 Sorley Boy was taken prisoner by his brother-in-law Shane O'Neill at the battle of Glentaisie but was freed two years later after both families sat down to a banquet called to negotiate his release. But his family had other plans. During the banquet Sorley Boy's family murdered Shane O'Neill and freed Sorley. In 1584 Sorley was subsequently recaptured by Queen Elizabeth 1's Lord Deputy of Ireland, Sir John Perrot. Sir John brought with him an army and forced the Castle of Dunluce into surrender. Sir John then appointed Peter Carey as constable of Dunluce Castle. This infuriated Queen Elizabeth and in 1586 handed back the Castle to Sorley Boy.

Sorley Boy undertook new buildings at Dunluce, particularly the Italian-style loggia and also announced his return to the castle by hanging Peter Carey from the ramparts of the south tower. Prior to his death in 1589 his sons, James and Randal, added to the fortifications, probably building the Scottish-style gatehouse around 1600. Randal, who became Viscount Dunluce, and 1st Earl of Antrim, founded a town west of the castle in 1620 and brought settlers from Scotland to live there. In 1635 Sorley Boy's grandson the 2nd Earl Randal married Catherine Manners, widow of George Villiers the Duke of Buckingham. The Earl built the Manor House, with its bay windows, for her and a new kitchen court on the rock. Despite this, the Duchess never liked Dunluce. In 1936 during a storm the north wall of the kitchen collapsed and fell into the stormy seas taking several of the castle's servants with it. That was enough for the Duchess. She insisted the family abandon the castle and build a house inland. The castle remained habitable for the remainder of the 17th century but because it no longer remained the seat of the McDonnell family it slowly fell into decline until the weather battered its walls into what we know today as Dunluce Castle.

The mainland court contains domestic buildings

leading downhill to the narrow crossing to the rock formerly protected by a drawbridge to the Gatehouse. The buildings on the rock almost all date to the 16th (early 17th) century. Slight earthworks visible to the west of the castle are remains of a formal garden and part of the long-deserted town whose ruined church stands in the graveyard south of the castle separated from it by the modern coast road.

Even though Dunluce Castle is a crumbling façade of its former glory its past occupants still see it as home. There have been several sightings of ghostly aspirations seen within the walls of the castle. A ghostly white lady who wanders the north-east tower is believed to be the spirit of the daughter of the family, who after her father refused to let her marry the man she loved died within the wall of the castle of a broken heart. There is also a ghostly

Dunluce Castle ruins

figure of a man wearing a purple cloak seen wandering the tower. He is believed to be the spirit of Peter Carey who was hanged by Sorley Boy. Staff and visitors to the castle have also reported feeling a cold chill come over them as they enter the south east tower even on the warmest of days and have felt a spirit brushing past them as if in a hurry. In the castle's shop staff have reported that books have been stacked on the floor from the shelves overnight and radios are mysteriously switched on.

Dunluce Castle is located on the North Antrim coast.

Dunluce Castle,
87 Dunluce Road,
Bushmills,
Co. Antrim
Phone: 048 20731938

Glenveagh Castle

The estate of Glenveagh was created in 1857-1859 by the purchase of several smaller holdings by John George Adair from Co. Laois. Adair was infamous throughout Donegal and Ireland for evicting some 244 tenants in the cold April of 1861.

Most of the evictions took place at the edge of the estate along the shore of Lough Gartan. Adair cared little for the souls of the families he evicted. Many of them made their way to Australia, while others found refuge with relatives or were forced into the workhouse.

John Adair built Glenveagh Castle in 1870, to the design of his cousin John Townsend's trench. Overlooking Lough Veagh, Glenveagh Castle stands atop a slight promontory jutting into the lake. Few buildings in Ireland can boast of as fine a setting. Made from rough-hewn granite, the castle is a castellated mansion. It consists of a four storey rectangular keep with walls 1½ metres thick, with battlemented ramparts, turrets and a round tower. Many of the rooms inside still have the furnishings of the last private owner Henry McIlhenny.

The castle was a crown for John Adair for his triumphant achievements and a home to his new bride, a wealthy American Cornelia Adair. No sooner had the castle been built than the couple spent most of their time in America, where Adair had interests in ranching and brokerage. John Adair died in St. Louis in 1885 and shortly after his wife returned to Glenveagh Castle. Cornelia survived until 1921 and unlike her husband is remembered as a kind and generous person who enhanced the castle by planting shelter belts and developing the grounds. The Castle was occupied by the IRA in 1922 but they evacuated it when the Free State Army approached. The building then served as an army garrison for three years, after which the glen returned to its tranquil ways.

Glenveagh fell into decline until its purchase in 1929 by Professor Arthur Kingsley Porter of Harvard. His stay was short, as he disappeared mysteriously from Inishbofin Island in 1933. The last private owner was Mr Henry McIlhenny of Philadelphia, USA, who bought the estate in 1937. In 1975, the lands of Glenveagh were purchased by the State and in 1981 Mr McIlhenny presented Glenveagh Castle and Gardens to the Irish nation, thereby adding greatly to the amenities of the National Park. Further land acquisitions have since been made to conserve areas of special natural value.

The gardens of the castle boast a multitude of exotic plants whose luxuriance contrasts starkly with the surrounding mountains. Work on the gardens began under the direction of Mrs Adair and the subsequent efforts of Henry McIlhenny and his advisors Jim Russell and Lanning Roper have resulted in gardens of extraordinary charm.

Glenveagh Castle

It was in 2004 when a visiting foreign musician played at the castle. He was given one of the rooms to change into his performing clothes. After his performance he retired to the room to change back into his normal clothes and was discovered some time later, half dressed, by members of the staff. He tried to explain in broken English that there was something or someone in the room with him as he was dressing and he refused to re-enter the room. Castle staff had to go into the room to retrieve the rest of his clothing. Nothing was seen or heard in the room by the staff while they were retrieving his clothing. One member of staff pointed out that although it was in the middle of summer and the rooms were not cold he could see goose bumps standing on the skin of the musician who was shaking with fright. Who or what the visiting musician saw we will never know but this event was witnessed by many staff members. Could it be the spirit of John Adair or his wife Cornelia who loved the castle very much, or could it be a spirit of some evicted peasant farmer kicked off his land by John Adair getting revenge in his own mischievous way?

Glenveagh Castle,
Church Hill,
Letterkenny,
Co. Donegal

Phone 074 37090

Grace Neill's

Grace Neill's first opened its doors in 1611 and was then known as the King's Arms. A 17th century visitor to the establishment, the Marquis de Vere, commented that good food and excellent ale were served there. When the poet John Keats visited Donaghadee he was impressed with how clean and charming the town was. But, the inhabitants of the town according to Keats were as rough and savage a bunch as he had ever seen in his life, especially the regulars at the King's Arms. It was within the walls of the pub that he was treated to ridicule, scorn and violent abuse by the local people who probably objected to his style of dress and thought he was some strange foreigner from England. Grace Neill was the proprietor from 1818 to 1916 and during this time was known as a lady full of character who liked to keep a commodious establishment and a watchful eye on proceedings while enjoying a smoke on her clay pipe. Grace greeted her guests to the pub with

PAUL FENNELL

a peck on the cheek. In 1842 when Grace was twenty-four she married John Neill who was only sixteen at the time. She gave birth to their first son William John Neill in 1844, but he sadly drowned at sea at the young age of thirty. He is buried at Morseby Church. Her second son Hugh Neill also fell to the "hungry sea" at the age of twenty-four on 10th November 1876. Her third son James died in August 1907. Grace had a fourth son Alec and a granddaughter by her son James who also died in 1882 at the age of two years and three months. When Grace died in 1916 she had outlived and sadly seen most of her family pass away. You can still visit the Neills' family grave at Donaghadee Cemetery. There are in total ten of the Neills buried in the family plot, the last member of the family, Agnes, being buried there in 1956 at the ripe old age of eighty-two.

Even though Grace died in 1916, her spirit still lives on ensuring that the hostelry that now bears her name continues to operate with the smooth efficiency that both Grace and her clients had come to expect. Several portraits of Grace hang from the wall and gaze down on the clientele of today. But it is the dark and cosy front bar which is said to have been constructed from old ships' timbers that has changed very little since Grace oversaw the running of the pub. Grace is said to still show herself today. Staff have reported appliances switching themselves on and off without anyone being near them. Unseen hands have moved glasses around as well as books. Ghostly footsteps have been heard in the rooms above and there have also been reports of a Victorian lady seen in and around the darker recesses, cloaked in a cloud of smoke. Some patrons have felt a cold presence around the staircase as if someone was walking past them. But Grace's spirit is not nasty, it is a kind-hearted spirit who is reported to still greet guests with a peck on the cheek, keeping up her tradition. Patrons and staff have nothing to fear from her as she is just popping by to make sure her establishment is being kept to her standards. So if you are entering Grace Neill's and you feel a gentle peck on the cheek, don't jump back in fear, but enter knowing that Grace has accepted you into her establishment in her own special way.

Grace Neill's,
33 High Street,
Donaghadee,
Co. Down,
Northern Ireland

Phone: 048 9188 4595

The Case of the Ghost
of Helena Blunden

The best place for researching information on ghosts and hauntings is the Internet. From here you can access information from all around the globe on most locations, but please take this information with a pinch of salt; not all of it is true, a lot of it is misleading and in one case an insult to the paranormal world. This case would be the story of the Ghost of Helena Blunden 1896-1912.

It is claimed that Helena Blunden was sixteen when she began her work in the spinning room of the linen mill in the old market area of Belfast. She was claimed to be the eldest daughter of a woman from Tyrone and her father was a Kilkenny man. Helena was born in Ireland but brought up in England after her parents moved there. In 1911, the Blundens returned to Ireland and chose Belfast as their new home. Their decision to return was supposed to be politically motivated. With the reform of the House of Lords in 1911, the Lords' power of veto over Home Rule was limited to a delaying tactic. The passage of a Home Rule Bill through Westminster was assured, which would grant Ireland a domestic parliament and allow a degree of political independence from England. Helena's father was an ardent Home Ruler. He would have preferred to settle in Dublin, but Helena's uncles on her mother's side had already arranged jobs for the Blundens in Belfast. The Blundens moved into their new home, a small terraced house in Raphael Street which was reported to be only a few hundred yards from the linen mill.

Helena is portrayed as a typical young Irish girl, a popular worker in the linen mill. A cheerful young woman, like all young women her head was full of the romanticism of Yeats' poetry and the songs of the London music halls. Her grand uncle had been a wandering Irish dancing master in Kilkenny. Helena was supposed to have inherited his talent for dance but she was more interested in singing than dancing. Since her return to Ireland it is reported that she had danced at Feiseanna in Dublin. Her father wanted to encourage her talent for the stage, but Helena's mother frowned upon this notion. While living in London Helena had grown up among the immigrant Irish there, but invented a peculiar English accent which impressed her fellow workers at the mill. Her aspirations and songs, her accent and memories of London always guaranteed her a captivated audience at the mill and she enjoyed all the attention.

Like all manual labour in the late 1800s to early 1900s the work in the spinning room was hard, arduous and repetitive. On warm days in summer when the heat reached boiling point, children and women would often faint. Margaret Maxwell also worked in the mill and was a tough woman who in her youth had brawled with both men and women in the streets of Belfast. Margaret had reached an old age and was no longer fit to fight or work in the flax room. So she was employed in the afternoons to mop and clean the condensation that built up on the stairs. Pride made Margaret resent this work but the necessity to make a living made her stay. She complained fiercely and scolded anyone who dared to walk on the stairs while she mopped them. She also frightened the young children, but the adults only scorned her threats. She would clash often with Helena, degrading the young woman's songs and hopes.

It is reported on ghostwatch@irelandseye.com that Helena worked sixty hours a week. On Saturdays when the working day was supposed to finish at 12 noon, the workers always stayed late when an important order had to be prepared. The linen companies where Helena worked produced double damask linen tablecloths. These tablecloths were laid on the tables in the first class dining room on the *Titanic*.

On Sunday 14th April 1912, the workers including the half timers in all departments came in to finish an order for Argentina. As always Helena was preoccupied with a concert she was due to attend in the Grand Opera House that evening. She sang her way through the morning and into the afternoon and evening. By 2pm, Helena realised that her work would not be complete before 6pm and that

301

there would not be much time between finishing her work at the mill and going to sing at the concert. Helena decided to keep her shoes on all day, ready to leave the minute her work at the mill was complete. Margaret Maxwell was already tired before she even began her work at the mill that day. Margaret, not in the mood for mopping the stairs, half-heartedly dabbled the mop along the top flight. She stopped to chastise a young half-timer who had only started and had not been warned about Margaret's stairs.

At 7pm, Helena finally finished her work at the mill. Already exhausted by the hard work and the summer heat, and with the excitement of the concert ahead that evening. Helena went down the first flight of stairs. She tripped on the discarded mop, fell over the banister and down to the ground floor. Margaret heard the shrieking Helena and looked up to watch Helena falling. Margaret released her grip on the young boy she was chastising and staggered down to the ground floor to discover that Helena was already dead. Helena's intention had been to leave the linen mill forever and establish herself as a singer. Of course she may never have succeeded as a singer and may have been destined to stay in the spinning room for years, reminiscing about the times she had sung on stage. Her death at sixteen dashed those aspirations.

There are reasonable, sensible men and women who say that Helena did not escape from the mill and that she still walks in that building. Some staff members have a theory that construction work being carried out in the building may have disturbed her spirit. A machine operator found a phonographic wax cylinder with a recording of

Helena singing. While attempting to extinguish a minor fire caused by building debris, he unearthed a mysterious bundle buried in sand in a century-old fire bucket. Wrapped in a piece of rough linen cloth were some scraps of paper, a wax recording cylinder, in almost perfect condition, and a key. Forensic examination of the cylinder deemed it a recording of Helena herself. Although the quality of the sound is very poor, a well-developed voice can be heard singing Pie Jesu from Fauré's Requiem.

This is the story of Helena Blunden as told on the website but if you examine this a little deeper you will find hidden clues that tell a different story. For, hidden within the text of the story are links that lead you to clues that reveal that the story is in fact a fake. If you go to the main ghost-watch page on the left hand side you will see a menu, click on the name Helena Blunden, this will take you to another page of text about her story. Scroll down until you come to the word Westminster and click on this word. Here you will find the clue "Run after it but not the one with the big live in the discovery". Now go back to the left hand side and click on The Linen Industry just under the name Helena Blunden. This will take you to a page titled The Irish Linen Industry. Scroll down this text until you come to the words War of the Worlds. Click on this and you are taken to another clue "the answer lies after the second hole in the linen worker's yarn". Now scroll down this page a little further until you come to the words Twentieth Century. Click on this and another clue is revealed "not unlike the setter but sure smells fishier the corridor". There are reported to be other clues, I have not been successful in finding them within the text but on the internet they are as follows: "Climb the way through Babylon and on to the sightings"; "Mount the gravel between the grass then the corridor"; "If the first is flesh and second fowl, it's the third in the discovery". They all apparently lead you back to the page titled "The Terrible Tragic Tale of Helena Blunden". Now move your mouse over these words and if you click each one in turn you are taken to a different irelandseye.com page. Now here is the secret, just move the mouse over the letter "T" in the word Tragic and this takes you to an "explorer user prompt" asking you a question. This is where the page telling you it is all a fake is kept.

I am not saying that Helena and her family did not live in Belfast and that Helena did not work or die in a linen mill. Nor am I saying that she did not die the very day the *Titanic* sank. The *Titanic* had been built in Harland and Wolff's Belfast shipyards within sight of where she worked. Helena, along with others in the mill had been employed only months earlier making tablecloths for the first class dining room on the doomed liner.

Since its birth millions of web surfers have joined in the great Irish ghost watch, hosted by Internet publisher Ireland's Eye and many visitors have reported seeing the ghost of a sixteen-year-old girl on a live web cam. The amazing story of The Great Irish Ghost Watch had only scheduled to take place over a one-week period during Halloween 1998. However, such was the interest and demand that it was installed on a permanent basis. I will allow you to draw your own conclusion.

Springhill House

The exact date of the construction of Springhill House is unknown but its origins go as far back as 1680 when "Good Will" Conyngham married his sixteen-year-old sweetheart Ann Upton. Her father was very anxious to ensure that she and any children she might have should be kept in the manner to which he felt that they should become accustomed. With that Ann Upton's father drew up a marriage contract. Part of this contract required Good Will to build a house of lime and stone, two storeys high with the necessary office, houses, gardens and orchards. Good Will rose to the challenge. He erected a handsome house which was lived in by subsequent generations of his family. In 1957 Captain William Lenox–Conyngham bequeathed Springhill and its contents to the National Trust.

The most paranormal part of Springhill House has to be the Blue Room.

In 1814 George Lenox-Conyngham was away on duty

in the army when he received news that his children were ill and diagnosed with smallpox. George was out of his mind with worry and awaited news of their conditions. But when no news reached him he abandoned his post early one night and headed for Springhill. On the way he met his commanding officer Robert Stewart. George explained his situation to Robert and felt sure that he would understand the urgency of his quest. Robert raised no objections and George made it back to Springhill where he found that his wife Olivia had nursed all the children back to health. But for George his relief was to be short-lived as he received the news that he was to be court-marshalled for abandoning his post. His so-called friend Robert had betrayed him. This news and the sudden death of one of his daughters sent George into a depression that lasted two years.

One fateful night George went downstairs to the gunroom, took one of his pistols from the wall, made his way into the blue room, sat on the side of the bed and shot himself. His wife Olivia realising what he was going to do ran down the corridor to stop him. She was too late, for just as she reached the bedroom door she heard the gun fire. George did not die straight away from his gun shot wound. It was two days after this fateful incident that George Lenox-Conyngham died. Olivia made a note in the family bible "George Lenox-Conyngham being in a very melancholy state of mind for many months prior, put an end to his existence by a pistol shot. He lingered from the 20th Nov. 1816 to the 22nd, and died, thanks to almighty God, a truly penitent Christian...'

The ghost of Olivia is still said to repeat the desperate dash to prevent her husband's death and she has been seen on several occasions standing at the door of the blue room with her hands raised in horror. This to me is a classic example of residual energy playing back a traumatic event in the history of this house.

In the latter part of the 19th century a houseguest, Miss Wilson, who had sat up late one night chatting with the daughter of the house Milly Conyngham claimed to have seen the ghost of Olivia. The story goes that when Milly retired to bed Miss Wilson noticed that she had left her diary behind. Leaving the room to return the diary to Milly she was startled by the sudden appearance of a tall woman at the top of the stairs. The apparition moved to a bedroom door, raised her arms apparently in despair and distress and then slowly faded away.

Some years later another guest of the house Miss Hamilton retired to bed one night in the Blue Room when just as she was starting to fall asleep she saw what appeared to be a roomful of agitated servants who were pushing and wrangling together in whispers. Lying in her bed terrified she heard a noise from the wall behind her bed and, turning slowly, saw a door open and a bright light shining in from it. She later recalled how someone seemed to come from this light and calmed the commotion among the servants. Miss Hamilton soon fell asleep after this strange but bizarre happening but on waking the next morning she was even more startled to find that no door existed anywhere behind her bed. However, when she reported her experience to Charlotte Lenox-Conyngham, she was told that there was in fact a door behind the bed but it had been papered over long ago. Some years later when the Blue Room was being redecorated the hidden door was revealed. It opened into a powder closet, and on the floor of this closet lay an old pair of gloves and a small pouch containing bullets for a gun.

It was in the early part of the 20th century the last generation of Lenox-Conyngham children lived at the house. One night while they slept their nursemaid suddenly awoke to find Olivia's phantom standing over the children gazing intently at them, as though checking to see that all was well with them. The nursemaid felt that they were in no danger at all, but in fact she was moved by how much concern the apparition appeared to show towards each of the Lenox-Conynham children. You will find if you ever visit Springhill House and are ever fortunate enough to sense the presence of any of the house's spirits, that there is nothing malevolent in this beautiful old house.

The National Trust,
Springhill,
Moneymore,
Magherafelt,
Co. Londonderry
Northern Ireland BT45 7NQ

Phone: 028 8674 8210.

A Final Note

When you were a young child alone at night in your bedroom you became frightened at strange shadows in the darkest corners of your room, you switched the light on and your fears went away. As you got older and watched horror films in the dark late at night and became frightened by them you switched the light on and your fears went away.

The fear of the paranormal is the same, nothing more that the fear of the unknown. For all those fears that you have pushed into the back of your mind of ghosts, demons and poltergeists that pop up again and again to haunt you in times of stress and torment, please use this book as your light. Knowledge and understanding is the key to ridding your life of the fear of the unknown. The more you understand the paranormal the more you will embrace this fascinating subject.

May the light of God shine on you and may your angels and spirits continue to guide you through your path in life.

Appendix

A special thank you to the following

- Paranormal Research Association of Ireland.
  www.praofi.org

- Office of Public Works.

- Lucan Library.

- Dublin Central Library.

- Walkinstown Library

- Pearse Street library.

- National Archives of Ireland.

- Fingal County Council.

- Tony and Geraldine McMahon of Johnnie Fox's Pub.

- Dudley Stewart and Bonnie Vance of Charleville
  Forest Castle.

- The staff of Springhill House and the National
  Trust for the use of the picture of the house.

- The staff of Drimnagh Castle.

- John Hoyne, manager of the Brazen Head Pub.

- William Kinsella and staff at Wicklow Historical Jail for their stories.

- To the staff and management of Castle Leslie for all their help and for permission to use their pictures of Castle Leslie.

- Ross Castle.

- To the staff of ThoorBallylee and Ireland West Tourism.

- To the owner and manager of Grace Neill's for his help with this project.

- Kinnitty Castle.

- To the staff and management of Malahide Castle.

- To the staff of Foulksrath Castle and the staff of An Oige youth hostels.

- To the staff and management of Ardgillan Castle.

- To the staff of Bantry House.

- Staff of McCarthys Pub.

- Staff of Renvyle House.

- Staff of King House.

- Staff of Huntington Castle.

- Staff of the Shelbourne Hotel.

- National Museum at Collins Barracks.

- St Michan's Church.

- Irish Press Plc.

- Áras an Uachtaráin.

- Dublin Castle.

- Marsh's Library.

- Portlick Castle.

- Glenveagh Castle for an amazing story.

- Dobbins Inn.

- Carrickfergus Castle.

- Appletree Press Ltd.

And to the staff at all of our national monuments who keep these national treasures so well preserved for all to enjoy.

I must give a special thanks to all ghosts, spirits and poltergeists that remain a part of our lives and who, for hundreds of years have intrigued our imagination with questions as to their very existence.